THE HOUSE BEAUTIFUL

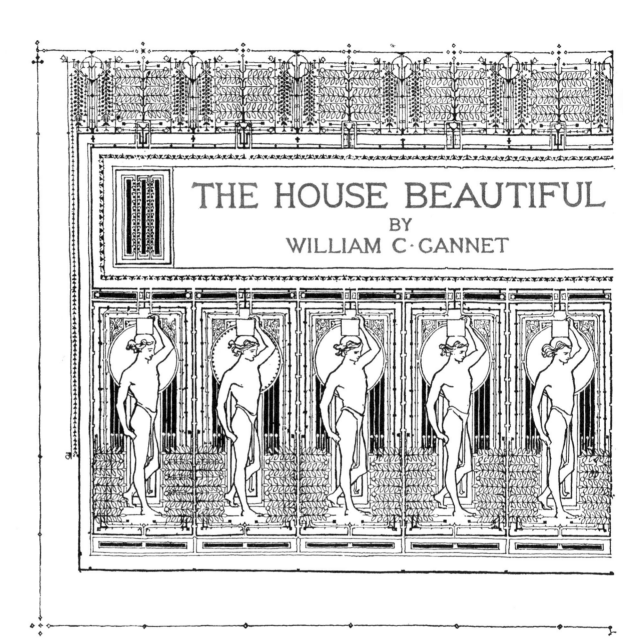

THE HOUSE BEAUTIFUL

BY
WILLIAM C·GANNET

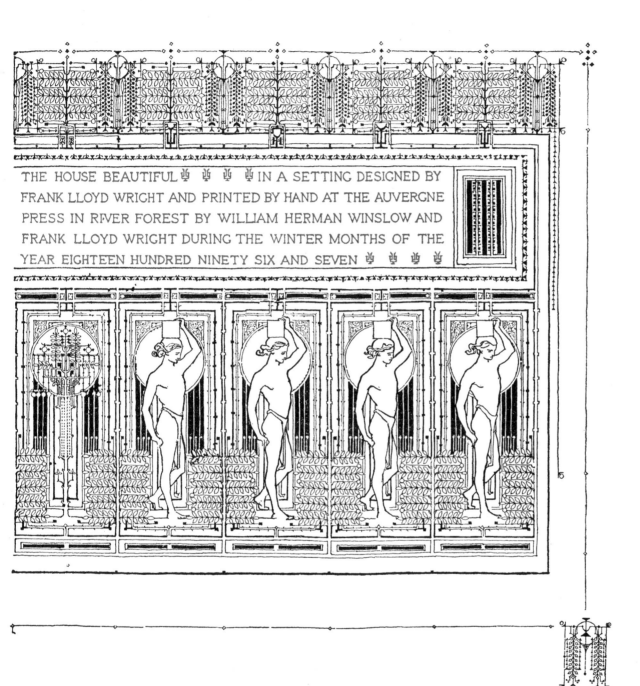

THE HOUSE BEAUTIFUL ⚜ ⚜ ⚜ ⚜ IN A SETTING DESIGNED BY
FRANK LLOYD WRIGHT AND PRINTED BY HAND AT THE AUVERGNE
PRESS IN RIVER FOREST BY WILLIAM HERMAN WINSLOW AND
FRANK LLOYD WRIGHT DURING THE WINTER MONTHS OF THE
YEAR EIGHTEEN HUNDRED NINETY SIX AND SEVEN ⚜ ⚜ ⚜ ⚜

Dedicated to Bruce Goff and America's visionary architects

Published by Pomegranate Artbooks
Box 6099, Rohnert Park, California 94927

Pomegranate Europe Ltd.
Fullbridge House, Fullbridge
Maldon, Essex CM9 7LE
England

Based on the original edition printed in 1898 by Frank Lloyd Wright
and William Herman Winslow.

Text © 1996 John Arthur
This edition © 1996 Pomegranate Artbooks

Library of Congress Cataloging-in-Publication data is on file
with the Library of Congress
Library of Congress Catalog Card Number 95-52960
IBSN 0-87654-597-5
Pomegranate Catalog No. A835

Printed in Korea

ACKNOWLEDGMENTS

For more than twenty years I have pursued the prospect of returning Frank Lloyd Wright's version of *THE HOUSE BEAUTIFUL* to print in an affordable edition. Over the last fifteen years various publishers have turned down proposals for everything from a lavish facsimile to an inexpensive paperback. Now, one hundred years after Wright and Winslow originally took up the endeavor, *THE HOUSE BEAUTIFUL* will be widely available for the first time. Rather than being an exercise in nostalgia or merely a piece of Frank Lloyd Wright memorabilia, the book takes on new shadings and quite different reverberations in our more jaded time.

Years ago I loaned my copy of *THE HOUSE BEAUTIFUL* to Bruce Goff. He always kept it next to *A System of Architectural Ornament,* a gift to him from Louis Sullivan. It was Goff who introduced me to the work of Greene and Greene and Bernard Maybeck at a time when most accounts of American architecture emphasized the import of the Bauhaus, International Style, and Museum of Modern Art, and contemporary art history reflected a strong bias toward Formalism. And it was Goff, the great radical of American architecture, who elaborated on the significance of the American bungalow for me and placed it in the context of the Arts and Crafts movement over lunch in a Bartlesville, Oklahoma, diner more than thirty years ago.

First, I want to salute Thomas Burke and Pomegranate Artbooks for recognizing the historic and esthetic import of *THE HOUSE BEAUTIFUL* and producing this handsome trade edition.

The Chicago architect William Hasbrouck graciously provided me with important background information on the original edition of *THE HOUSE BEAUTIFUL.* Margaret Klinkow and the Frank Lloyd Wright Home and Studio Foundation Research Center were extremely generous in sharing their notes and pertinent articles and fielding my phone calls.

Richard Howard readily solved the mystery of the unidentified poetry in the original version, and Jonathan Aaron met with me several times to discuss the long-ignored Gannett essay and the pieces by Wright and Winslow. He also helped place the writings in the context of their time.

Wendy Watson, Curator of the Mount Holyoke Museum, steered me to various resources in this area, and through her I was directed to David Dempsey, Preparator-Conservator of the Smith College Museum of Art, and the photographer and gravure printer Jon Goodman. The former identified the papers used in the original book, and the latter resolved the nagging puzzle of the reproductive process used for Wright's photographs.

Once again, Midori Shiraishi provided me much pertinent information. Like the journalist Lafcadio Hearn, Wright is revered in Japan, but his work takes on quite different reverberations when observed from the perspective of Japan's ancient culture. Not only did Shiraishi-san cast light on the Japanese view of his work, she translated the old pictographs carved into Wright's ivory seal, a souvenir from his first trip to Japan.

The biographical material on William C. Gannett and Jenkin Lloyd Jones was supplied by The Unitarian Universalist Society of Amherst, Massachusetts.

Last, my editor, Betty Childs, has once again deftly rearranged the content and removed much of the awkwardness from a rather densely packed foreword. For more than fifteen years she has worked her subtle magic on my manuscripts, an unheralded endeavor that can be fully appreciated only by other writers.

—J. A.

And the book is becoming to you and to me what the cathedral was to the Middle Ages. It enbalms for us in type the qualifications of our time.

Frank Lloyd Wright, 1896[1]

Frank Lloyd Wright was twenty-eight years old when he and William H. Winslow began their collaboration on *THE HOUSE BEAUTIFUL* in the winter of 1896. Their endeavor centered on an extremely popular and widely circulated essay by the distinguished Unitarian minister William C. Gannett, which had been published a year earlier as an inexpensive pamphlet. Wright and Winslow's extravagantly produced volume was printed in an edition of ninety copies and took three years to complete. It is one of the most beautiful books published during the American Arts and Crafts movement.

That final decade of the nineteenth century was distinguished by monumental scientific accomplishments, far-reaching industrial inventiveness, and brilliant esthetic endeavors.

By 1896 the most advanced art and architecture in Europe and America was marked by the influence of the Far East, and by the overlapping esthetic principles of Art Nouveau, which was a rejection of academic historicism, and the Arts and Crafts movement, with its advocacy of high craft and design reform.

In Vienna Gustav Klimt submitted the studies for his monumental panels representing *Philosophy, Medicine,* and *Jurisprudence* for Vienna University's Great Hall. By the time Wright and Winslow finished printing and binding their edition of *HOUSE BEAUTIFUL* three years later, the Vienna Secession had been founded by Klimt, Otto Wagner, Josef Maria Olbrich, Josef Hoffmann, and Koloman Moser, and Olbrich's stately Secession Exhibition Building, with its leafy gilded dome, had been erected. Wright and Olbrich both were born in 1867, and both architects distinguished themselves at a young age. In a relationship similar to Wright's with Louis Sullivan, Olbrich was a protégé of Otto Wagner. Early in his career, when Wright's handsome, modern residences first appeared in European publications, he was described as an "American Olbrich." Unfortunately, unlike Wright, whose career spanned more than seven decades, Olbrich would die at the age of forty-one.

In Vésinet, France, the Villa la Hublotiere, a beautiful Art Nouveau residence designed by Hector Guimard, had just been constructed, and in Paris the intimist painter Edouard Vuillard installed his lavishly patterned, tapestry-like cycle of four paintings, *Figures and Interiors,* in the library of Marcel Proust's physician, Marcel Vaquez.

In Spain, for more than a decade Antonio Gaudi had been supervising the work on his Sagrada Familia in Barcelona. (Years later Wright would sarcastically describe this visionary structure as architecture with diarrhea.[2])

In England, C. F. A. Voysey completed the perfectly proportioned, stucco-clad Norney, a residence that easily equaled the best of Wright's achievements of that period. Edwin Lutyens and Gertrude Jekyll had begun their house and garden collaboration, and in 1897 Lutyens designed Munstead Wood, a rustic cottage in the English vernacular tradition, for her.

Wright immediately recognized that Jekyll's informal garden designs, so much a part of the English Arts and Crafts movement, would revolutionize landscape architecture. In a lecture given in 1900 he would praise her just-published book, *Home and Garden,* in which she described her lovely cottage garden.[3] But true to form, he did not acknowledge Lutyens, her well-known collaborator, nor would he ever publicly mention the architecture of the highly respected Voysey.

To the north in Scotland Charles Rennie Mackintosh was drawing the plans for the first phase of the Glasgow School of Art and beginning work on the airy Art Nouveau interiors of Miss Cranston's Tea Rooms.

And last, in 1896 the contentious, overbearing, and brilliant William Morris died. More than any other individual, he had forged the social, philosophical, and esthetic underpinnings of the Arts and Crafts movement in England and America. The last major publication of his Kelmscott Press was a lavish edition of the *Works of Geoffrey Chaucer* with illustrations by Morris's close friend, the Pre-Raphaelite painter Edward Burne-Jones. Completed a few months before his death, it had taken four years to produce.

Frank Lloyd Wright and his American contemporaries were quite familiar with the work of the Secessionists in Vienna and of the major English Arts and Crafts architects Voysey, M. H. Baillie Scott, E. S. Prior, and Lutyens, and with the work of their progenitor William Morris as well as the Glasgow designs of Mackintosh, through various contemporary books, periodicals, and international expositions. (Conversely, the brilliant architectural designs of Sullivan and Wright were acknowledged quite early in England and Europe.)

In America, after completing the Guaranty Building in 1895, the partnership of Dankmar Adler and Louis Sullivan had been dissolved. The following year, just as Wright and Winslow were beginning their publishing venture, Sullivan wrote his most important treatise, "The Tall Office Building Artistically Considered." His career had begun its tragic decline. However, for Wright, this period was a productive, efflorescent time. In just three brief years after his heated departure from the firm of Adler & Sullivan the young architect had designed and supervised the construction of twelve homes, a boathouse, a rowhouse, a windmill, a baptismal font, and four apartment buildings, and had remodeled several residences. Wright's first major commission after leaving Adler & Sullivan was the elegantly proportioned, wide-eaved home and stable for his friend and future collaborator and his wife, Mr. and Mrs. William Winslow, in River Forest, Illinois.

In 1896 Wright designed the Romeo and Juliet Windmill, a picturesque, romantic folly whose only function was to pump water to his aunts' school, and the Isidore Heller residence, a chunky, fortress-like house with an elaborate sculptural frieze by Richard Bock (strikingly similar to Wright's title page for the Auvergne Press edition of *The Eve of St. Agnes*), but with the exception of the Joseph and Helen Husser residence of 1899, Wright's architecture would not take on its characteristic horizontality until after the turn of the new century.

By this time the entwined esthetics of Art Nouveau, Arts and Crafts, and Orientalism were reflected from coast to coast in the most progressive American art and architecture.

Bernard Maybeck had built the first of his rustic cottages in the hills surrounding Berkeley, California, by 1896, but it would be another five years before the brothers Charles Sumner and Henry Mather Greene would connect with tenets of the Arts and Crafts movement through the influence of articles in Will Bradley and Gustav Stickley's *Craftsman* magazine. They would move the architecture of the American bungalow into the realm of high art.

The social and cultural chasm separating the unpretentious Arts and Crafts residences by Wright, Greene and Greene, and Maybeck from the rambling châteaux and ostentatious Beaux Arts mansions built by America's scions of commerce and industry on the East Coast was succinctly described by George Sand when she said that "people could be classified according to whether they aspired to live in a cottage or a palace."[4]

During these years, while John Singer Sargent's elegant, seductively sumptuous portraits were in great demand by the upper tiers of American society, the Orientalist Arthur Wesley Dow, a major figure in the Arts and Crafts movement, was making highly simplified, schematic woodcut images which were inked with transparent watercolors as was the practice in Japan. His famous 1895 poster for the periodical *Modern Art* attests to the advanced nature of the movement. Dow's *Composition*, first published in 1899, and his pedagogical ideas would dominate art education in America for more than half a century.

The first examples of Louis Comfort Tiffany's iridescent *Favrile* glass appeared on the market in 1896. In the south, George Ohr, the "mad potter of Biloxi," was throwing his thin-walled and wildly inventive "mud babies" while boasting that he was the "unequaled-unrivaled-undisputed-greatest-art potter on the earth." Unfortunately, few agreed at the time, and he spent the last years of his life working as an auto mechanic.

At the end of the nineteenth century a large segment of the American public were avid readers, and their grasp of history and the arts, and the quantity and quality of the books and periodicals they read, far surpassed that of most readers today. Consequently, there was a proliferation of small presses during this period. The printing shop set up by William H. Winslow was one of these.

Winslow, the president of a highly successful ornamental ironwork firm, was a skilled craftsman and an amateur typographer and printer. To accommodate his avocation, Wright provided space for a press and workshop in his stable. Adopting the name of his street, Winslow called the small shop the Auvergne Press. Wright designed the printer's device, a shield with overlapping W's signifying the collaboration of Winslow, Wright, and their friend Chauncey Williams, a partner in the Chicago publishing house of Way and Williams.

Their first endeavor, *The Eve of St. Agnes* by John Keats, was printed earlier in 1896. Keats's poetry was held in high regard in England and America and was frequently published in handsome editions by small presses domestically and abroad. Wright drew the elaborate title page for the small volume, and it was printed in an edition of sixty-five.[5]

Wright and Winslow's second and final collaboration was *THE HOUSE BEAUTIFUL*. The Reverend William C. Gannett's name was misspelled (Gannet) on the title page, and apparently Williams was no longer involved. However, after the completion of *THE HOUSE BEAUTIFUL* Winslow would continue to print small, non-commercial books and pamphlets under the Auvergne Press imprint.

Like the Keats edition, this beautifully designed and exquisitely crafted volume reflects the Art Nouveau and Arts and Crafts movements. Neither book was made as a commercial endeavor. They were given to relatives, friends, and colleagues.

Gannett, the son of a leading Unitarian minister in Boston, graduated from Harvard Divinity School in 1868. Guided by a fierce social conscience, he was an abolitionist and an early proponent of non-creedal and anti-supernaturalist religion. After moving to the Midwest, Gannett became a close friend and associate of Wright's uncle, the well-known Chicago minister Jenkin Lloyd Jones. Both men were noted for their religious and social liberalism.

In 1886 Gannett referred to Wright (no doubt in an act of nepotism) as "the boy architect" assisting the noted J. Lyman Silsbee with the Jones family's shingle style chapel. This was the first written notice of Frank Lloyd Wright's involvement in architecture.

Gannett's writing skill and poetic bent served him well as a pamphleteer. His 1887 treatise "The Things Most Commonly Believed To-Day Among Us" articulated the basis for Unitarian unity and summed up liberal religion at the end of the nineteenth century.[6]

Without doubt Wright and Winslow's selection of Gannett's *HOUSE BEAUTIFUL* was based both on their admiration for the famous minister and on the broad appeal of his essay. For Wright there was also Gannett's long and close association with his uncle. After his essay first appeared as an inexpensive pamphlet in 1895 it was frequently reprinted. By 1899 various editions of the treatise had sold more than 10,000 copies, and it remained in print until 1928.[7]

At the time Gannett wrote this piece, "the house beautiful" was a widely used term. As Margaret Klinkow, former director of the Frank Lloyd Wright Home and Studio Foundation Research Center, has pointed out, the maxim appeared as early as 1678 in John Bunyan's *Pilgrim's Progress*. Later it was used by Calvert Vaux, and in 1877 the American art critic Clarence Cook wrote a book titled *The House Beautiful: Essays on Beds and Tables, Stools and Candlesticks*. The phrase was also incorporated in literary pieces by Oscar Wilde and Mark Twain, and was used in a poem by Robert Louis Stevenson.[8] In 1897 the periodical *House Beautiful*, using the title of Gannett's essay, began publication as a vehicle for the Arts and Crafts movement and claimed to be the "only magazine in America devoted to Simplicity, Economy, and Appropriateness in the home."[9]

Unlike the very modern, abstract setting designed by Wright, the timbre of the text is very much an expression of the period. Today, Gannett's tone strikes one as too ministerial, the mood as too sentimental, and his prose seems overwrought and flossy. However, the pertinence of the content of his treatise remains sound. The ethical, esthetic, and practical benefits he ascribes to the house beautiful—the lasting effects of good construction and comfortable furnishing, the enhancement of a room by beautiful objects, the charm and cheer brought into it by plants and flowers, the pedagogical and humanitarian role of good books and periodicals, the importance of graciousness, civility, and hospitality, and last, that spiritual fulfillment and emotional stability are best obtained through familial love—are too seldom mentioned today, but remain just as relevant in our time.

Just as a sermon is punctuated with scriptural verse, Gannett sprinkles his essay with poetry. With the exception of a phrase from Ralph Waldo Emerson, he quotes *To Lucasta, Going to the Wars* by the seventeenth-century English royalist and indelible phrasemaker Richard Lovelace, and draws from the poetry of Christina Rossetti, sister of the Pre-Raphaelite painter Dante Gabriel Rossetti.[10]

No doubt the author's appraisal of photography in the third chapter expressed the prevailing attitude in 1895, but it was a dreadfully skewed and unenlightened evaluation. Basically Gannett regards the medium, little more than a half century old, as no more than an inexpensive method for reproducing art, and states, ". . . it needs no mint of money to have really choice pictures on one's wall, now that photography has been invented, and the sun shines to copy Raphael's Madonna and Millet's Peasants. . . ."

At this time, during the height of America's upper class pre-tax ostentation, excesses, and social indifference, Gannett's ethical beliefs and politics were quite radical. His call to live simply and graciously and to act with generosity, combined with his admonitions against material excesses, traces back to the Transcendentalism of Henry David Thoreau and Ralph Waldo Emerson. But Gannett's praise for refinement and craftsmanship mixed with socialist reform must also be recognized as an expression of the ideals articulated earlier by William Morris. These same principles were at the center of the writing of Gustav Stickley and of Wright's friend Elbert Hubbard, and they provided an ethic and esthetic cornerstone for the shops of Candice Wheeler and Gustav Stickley, the pottery studios of the Saturday Evening Girls, Rookwood, and Teco, the architecture of Bernard Maybeck, Greene and Greene, and Frank Lloyd Wright, and the commonplace American bungalow as well. Much more than being a stylistic expression, the social and ethical connotations of the movement defined a way of life.

᭜ ᭜ ᭜ ᭜

Frank Lloyd Wright drew the elaborate linear enclosures for the six chapters of Gannett's essay and assisted Winslow in setting type and printing THE HOUSE BEAUTIFUL. Rather than attempting to reproduce the delicate drawings through the labor-intensive method of wood engraving, as was the practice for William Morris's books and other limited editions, metal plates were made using the relatively new process of electrotype.[11] This quietly marked an ideological break with the Arts and Crafts movement which would culminate in Wright's famous Hull House speech, "The Art and Craft of the Machine," given in 1901.[12]

Even though the title page states that the book was produced between 1896 and 1897, the project was not actually completed until 1898.[13] Excluding Wright and Winslow's long hours of labor, the production cost (photogravures, electroplates, paper, binding, etc.) was $6.00 per book.[14] This would be roughly the equivalent of $120.00 today.

While his graphic design and early renderings give proof of the young architect's brilliance, they also provide strong evidence that genius must be combined with an indomitable will. A decade after he made that clumsy, amateurish drawing for J. Lyman Silsbee's Unity Chapel,[15] Frank Lloyd Wright had evolved into a draftsman and designer of great skill, originality, and imagination.

To place the highly abstract drawings for THE HOUSE BEAUTIFUL in the context of the graphic art of their time, one should keep in mind that representations of plants and flowers in most of William Morris's wallpapers were quite literal, and while the book illuminations and illustrations for Morris's Kelmscott Press, Hubbard's Roycroft Print Shop, Jane Addams's Hull House, and the Wiener Werkstatte were stylized, they were always specific and recognizable. Henri Matisse, roughly the same age as Wright, was then struggling with dark, academic still life paintings, and Kandinsky would not completely abandon representational painting until 1910. The spare geometry of the windows Wright designed for the Avery Coonley house (1908) predated Mondrian's gridded abstractions by a decade.

Clearly these freehand designs show the influence of Louis Sullivan's drawings, reliefs, and stencil ornamentation, but they also reflect Wright's brilliant, virtuoso ability to fuse elements of the Wiener Werkstatte, Art Nouveau, English and American Arts and Crafts, Japanism, and his affection for Oriental rugs[16] into a harmonious, timeless, and deeply personal expression. The linear fretwork of these boxes can best be described as borders and fills, the basic design components of Middle Eastern tribal weaving. The text is set within these frames and the elaborate fill is used to return the chapters to the left page.

However, the generous margins are distinctly an architect's decision and demonstrate a clear break from book design of the period. The size of the heavy handmade paper, watermarked Whatman 1896, dictated the 13½ x 11 inch format. The pages were printed four to a sheet and cut in half horizontally, and the trimmed margin was goldleafed. Atypical of the nineteenth century, Wright's design relates to the double page spread rather than to the individual page. The filigreed boxes are positioned close to the gutter with wide, carefully proportioned borders at the edges. The effect is like a matted diptych. This airiness is consistent with the strong sense of fluidity and openness obtained in his later architecture through the elimination of interior walls, the angular, geometrical grouping of furniture within a room, and the slightly fractured but uninterrupted flow of space the architect gained through the predominant use of clear, beveled glass in his windows. Again, Wright's uncanny and extremely eloquent use of balance and proportion is more Oriental than Western.

Also serving as a reminder that this is an architect's work is Wright's choice of stock for the endsheets and cover. The boards were covered with the same mellow green paper used for the endsheets, with a one-third leather spine. Both W. R. Hasbrouck, architect and editor of the old *Prairie School Review,* and the late Bruce Goff stated that this stock was manufactured in rolls and used for covering drafting tables.

Connecting with Gannett's references to nature, Wright draws symbolic parallels in his title page spread, chapter designs, and photogravures of weeds and in the poems selected to precede the minister's text.

While all of the designs contain stylized abstractions of natural forms, the widely reproduced full title page, with its row of caryatids supporting a pergola,[17] is the most architectural. Unlike their wet-draped Delphic precedents, Wright's repeated male figure with its prudishly covered groin appears to have been copied from Cellini's statue of *Perseus.* Now helmetless, each figure balances a simple cubic capital on his head and supports a frieze containing the book's title and copy, and the espaliered rows of vines at the base are repeated above the title block. In the enclosure to the right of the gutter the figure has metamorphosed into an abstract foliated column. This illustration and the occasional inclusion of plaster casts of the *Nike of Samothrace* and *Aphrodite of Melos* in Wright's interiors typify the architect's sly, rare nods toward classical orders.

Characteristic of many books from this period are the red accents on the title page, in the ornamental devices, and the borders around the photographs in *THE HOUSE BEAUTIFUL.* This particular hue, often referred to as Renaissance red, was reportedly brought to Europe by Marco Polo. It is the color of the dough-like cinnabar ink used in affixing Japanese seals, which Wright would have known from prints and paintings. The architect's first Celtic cross logo, the unadorned red square used later in his books, the initialed square seen on his renderings, and the signed ceramic tile used on some of the buildings clearly indicate the architect's attractions to these beautiful stamps. In fact, he marked the books in his library with an ivory seal obtained on his first trip to Japan in 1905. It contains his phoneticized name (*ra-i-to in,* or Wright's seal) in a beautiful, ancient form of Kanji. Unfortunately, unable to read these pictographs, Wright used the seal upside down.[18]

Without question one of the most distinctive aspects of *THE HOUSE BEAUTIFUL* is the booklet of twelve photogravures by Wright, the unique means he devised for incorporating photography in the book as well as the ramifications of the photographs themselves.

Like many others at the turn of the century, the architect was attracted to this relatively new medium.

A proficient amateur, he used the camera to record his family life, to document the ongoing changes in his Oak Park home and studio, and to photograph plants and flowers. Wright's affinity for flora is reflected in his frequent use of concrete urns on the porches and walks of his early residences and in the various weed holders, ceramic pots, and copper urns he designed during this period. Unlike Gannett, the architect and others in the Arts and Crafts movement shared the pictorialists' opinion that photography was a new art form rather than a mimetic means for copying or imitating painting. The booklet of photogravures, like the Celtic cross and red square, also illustrates the seductive lure of Japan.

Wright first saw Japanese prints in the studio and home of J. Lyman Silsbee, which was filled with Oriental ceramics and art. The famous Orientalist Ernest Francisco Fenollosa, an early champion of *ukiyo-e* who had lived and taught in Japan, was Silsbee's cousin. It is likely that Wright met this distinguished scholar and lecturer in Silsbee's home during the time of his Chicago lectures.[19]

One can quickly grasp the stunning impact of Japanese prints in the late nineteenth century by comparing a Hiroshige woodcut with a Winslow Homer wood engraving for *Harper's Weekly*. European and American prints were monochromatic or hand colored. Graphic artists strove to achieve the specificity, tonal range, and naturalism of painting, and they adhered to Western compositional conventions. In sharp contrast, *ukiyo-e* prints were multi-colored, audaciously composed, and elaborately patterned, and the images were reduced to their descriptive essentials. Wright became a passionate collector and an authority on Japanese prints and acknowledged them as a major influence on his work.[20]

Beyond the obvious influence of Sullivan, Wright's images of weeds and wildflowers and his decorative borders obviously reflect the attitudes espoused earlier in Owen Jones's *Grammar of Ornament*, Viollet-le-Duc's *Discourses*, and Christopher Dresser's *Principles of Decorative Design*.[21] More importantly, they provide what is probably the earliest direct evidence of the influence of Japanese art on his work.

As Julia Meech has observed,[22] not only are the twelve photogravures strikingly similar to some of Hiroshige's flowers, they are in the format of his small *tanzaku* prints (literally, *tanzaku* is a long vertical tablet of decorative paper used for composing haiku poetry). Also, Wright's depictions of the delicate linear forms of weeds and flowers silhouetted against a plain background bear a strong resemblance to Oriental brush painting,[23] and while his compositions do not conform to the ancient, highly refined art of Japanese flower arrangement, they could be described as a Westernized form of ikebana.

Frequently these photogravures have been described as collotypes, but that is a planographic process similar to lithography. Jon Goodman, an authority on photogravure, examined the prints and concluded that Wright used a process called "dust ground gravure." As can be seen in the detail, it is technically derived from aquatint etching. These gravures are pulled on *mitsumata*, a thin, tough Japanese paper with ragged margins.[24] The red letterpress borders printed on their reverse sides are visible through the translucent paper used in the original edition. The last six borders incorporate Wright's Celtic cross.

This booklet of gravures is affixed to the front flyleaf of *THE HOUSE BEAUTIFUL*, with Shakespeare's sonnet "But flowers distill'd . . ." printed in gold on its cover.

The poems chosen by Frank Lloyd Wright and William H. Winslow have been identified by the poet and translator Richard Howard as Shakespeare's fifth and sixth sonnets and "Flower in the Crannied Wall" by Alfred, Lord Tennyson. These pieces, widely known at the turn of the century and obviously reflecting cultivated reading at that time, were selected to complement Gannett's inspirational text. Significantly, they also express the idealism of the Arts and Crafts movement.

Both William H. Winslow and Wright wrote introductory pieces for the Auvergne Press edition. Corresponding to their division of labor, Winslow addresses the production and printing of the book while Wright waxes poetic about the enhancement of Gannett's text through his illuminations. It is evident that both men, like the Reverend Gannett, believed that esthetic matters had ethical and spiritual ramifications.

Their pieces are given low marks for literary merit by Richard Howard. His evaluation is shared by the poet Jonathan Aaron, who described their efforts as being a cut above doggerel but rather typical of the poetry submitted to newspapers and periodicals at the turn of the century.

In 1902 Wright inscribed the Tennyson poem on a terra cotta nude that stands in the entrance of the Dana house in Springfield, Illinois. This figure holds severely angular, stylized flowers like those in his *HOUSE BEAUTIFUL* drawings. Linear abstractions of sumac plants and butterflies also similar to the plant and floral forms in the book are repeated in the windows and ornamentation throughout this residence, which is the most opulently decorated of all his Prairie School houses. Drawing such parallels to nature continued throughout Frank Lloyd Wright's long career.

In an early essay, "Architect, Architecture, and Client," written while Wright was working on *THE HOUSE BEAUTIFUL,* the architect stated, "These homes will be biographies and poems instead of slanderers and poetry crushers, appealing to the center of the human soul through perceptive faculties as potent as those that made the book."[25] His words are prophetic, for the freestanding, individual residence would remain at the center of Wright's oeuvre, and he never wavered in his opinion that the written word was a force even more powerful than architecture.

Today, almost four decades after his death, admiration for Frank Lloyd Wright's architecture is far greater than it was during his long, illustrious career, and there is no hint that this will abate. At the close of our scarred century, so lacking in idealism, authentic heroes, and ambitious, deeply resonating creative endeavor, Wright's estimate of his stature, ". . . not only do I intend to be the greatest architect who has yet lived, but the greatest who will ever live . . . ,"[26] seems less farfetched and even a bit less arrogant as we look back over the full range of his monumental achievements.

While *THE HOUSE BEAUTIFUL* has been frequently mentioned in the literature on Frank Lloyd Wright, it has sadly remained in the periphery of those discussions due to its extreme rareness and inaccessibility. This has been unfortunate, for the book provides an important key to the romantic and deeply humanistic concerns that lie at the heart of Frank Lloyd Wright's architecture.

For the first time Wright's original design, the full group of his photogravures, and the complete poetry and text have been united in an inexpensive format. This edition has been produced from the copy of *THE HOUSE BEAUTIFUL* that Wright presented to his uncle, the Reverend Jenkin Lloyd Jones.

For the architect, historian, and scholar, the treatise casts light into yet another early crevice in Wright's career, adding one more clue to the comprehension of the mercuric life of this complex master of American art and letters. But perhaps the most positive effect of reprinting *THE HOUSE BEAUTIFUL* at the close of our very different century is the chance that it will once again remind us of the true import of the home, garden, and family.

JOHN ARTHUR

NOTES

1. Bruce Brooks Pfeiffer, ed., *Frank Lloyd Wright: Collected Writings,* vol. 1 (New York: Rizzoli, 1992), p. 29.

2. Wright's appraisal was relayed to this writer by Bruce Goff, who greatly admired Gaudi's architecture.

3. Pfeiffer, *Wright: Collected Writings,* p. 56.

4. Quoted by Gaston Bachelard, *The Poetics of Space* (Boston: Beacon Press, 1969), p. 63.

5. Mary Jane Hamilton, *Frank Lloyd Wright and the Book Arts* (Madison: Friends of the University of Wisconsin–Madison Libraries, Inc., 1993), p. 47.

6. David Robinson, *The Unitarians and Universalists* (Westport, Conn.: Greenwood Press, n.d.), pp. 226–227.

7. Hamilton, *Wright and the Book Arts,* p. 62.

8. Margaret Klinkow, "The Wright Family in the House Beautiful," lecture notes (Oak Park, Ill.: Frank Lloyd Wright Home and Studio Foundation, 1991).

9. Wendy Kaplan, *The Art That Is Life: The Arts and Crafts Movement in America, 1875–1920* (Boston: New York Graphic Society), p. 298.

10. Most discussions of *THE HOUSE BEAUTIFUL* have completely ignored its text and poetry. This writer sent the poems to Richard Howard, one of the most distinguished and erudite poets in America. He identified them quite easily. In addition, the author discussed Gannett's essay, etc., with the poet and writer Jonathan Aaron. The photogravures were examined by Jon Goodman, a well-known photographer and photogravure printer who has conducted workshops on the process throughout the country.

11. Hamilton, *Wright and the Book Arts,* letter from Wright to Gannett, p. 64.

12. Pfeiffer, *Wright: Collected Writings,* pp. 58–69.

13. Hamilton, *Wright and the Book Arts,* p. 63.

14. Ibid., p. 64.

15. William Allin Storrer, *The Frank Lloyd Wright Companion* (Chicago and London: University of Chicago Press, 1993), drawing reproduced on p. 3. This is without question one of the most essential references on Wright.

16. David A. Hanks, *The Decorative Designs of Frank Lloyd Wright* (New York: Dutton, 1979), p. 174.

17. This author finds David Hanks's description of the title page drawing as depicting Apollonian figures walking through a landscape quite unconvincing, especially if one considers its various architectural elements and the wide use of pergolas in Arts and Crafts architecture. Also, this double page spread bears a striking compositional resemblance to the rows of figures in the *Egyptian Book of the Dead.*

18. Translated for the author by Midori Shiraishi, Yokohama, Japan.

19. Kevin Nute, *Frank Lloyd Wright and Japan* (New York: Van Nostrand Reinhold, 1993), pp. 22–27. In the flood of Frank Lloyd Wright literature over the last decade, this book is certainly one of the most pertinent. It contains an abundance of fresh material on Wright's connection with Japan and the profound influence of Japanese architecture and art on his residences and renderings.

20. Pfeiffer, *Wright: Collected Writings,* pp. 116–125.

21. Hanks, *Decorative Designs,* p. 2.

22. Julia Meech, *Japonisme Comes to America: The Japanese Impact on the Graphic Arts* (New York: Abrams, 1990), p. 74.

23. Pointed out in a letter to the author from Midori Shiraishi.

24. The various papers used in *THE HOUSE BEAUTIFUL* were examined by David Dempsey, Preparator-Conservator of the Smith College Museum of Art, Northampton, Massachusetts.

25. Pfeiffer, *Wright: Collected Writings,* p. 29.

26. Quoted in Peter Blake, *Frank Lloyd Wright: Architecture and Space* (Baltimore: Penguin Books, 1965), p. 95.

"BUT FLOWERS DISTILL'D, THOUGH THEY WITH WINTER MEET,
 LEESE BUT THEIR SHOW: THEIR SUBSTANCE STILL LIVES SWEET."
 WILLIAM SHAKESPEARE, SONNET 5

"THEN LET NOT WINTER'S RAGGED HAND DEFACE
 IN THEE THY SUMMER, ERE THOU BE DISTILL'D;
 MAKE SWEET SOME VIAL; TREASURE THOU SOME PLACE
 WITH BEAUTY'S TREASURE ERE IT BE SELF-KILL'D."
 WILLIAM SHAKESPEARE, SONNET 6

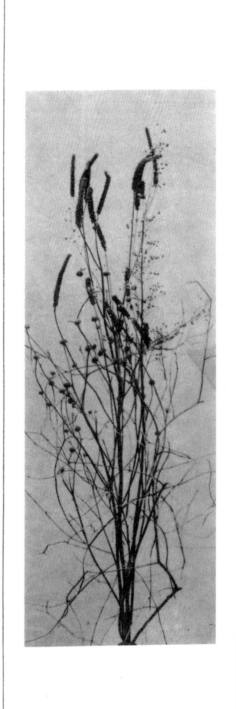

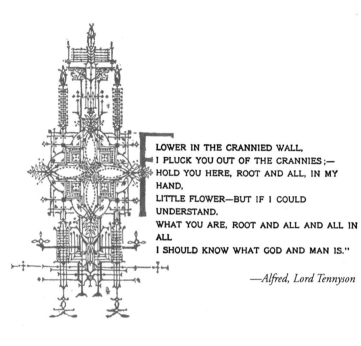

FLOWER IN THE CRANNIED WALL,
I PLUCK YOU OUT OF THE CRANNIES;—
HOLD YOU HERE, ROOT AND ALL, IN MY HAND,
LITTLE FLOWER—BUT IF I COULD UNDERSTAND.
WHAT YOU ARE, ROOT AND ALL AND ALL IN ALL
I SHOULD KNOW WHAT GOD AND MAN IS."

—*Alfred, Lord Tennyson*

HE MODERN EYE WITH CLEARER LIGHT SURVEYS
AND THEN DEMANDS A GREATER HARMONY;
THE TOUCH OF REASON, LOGIC,—ALL UNBEND,—
AND FIRED WITH SYMPATHY, AROUSE A FRESH
INCENSE OF SPIRIT, FREE AND FAIR; UNTRAMMELLED.
AND SO WE FASHION THE PRINTER'S SERIOUS ART
AND NEWLY WED THE THOUGHT WITH VISION'D TEXT.
A DAINTY TREND FOR BOOK AND PAGE AND PEN;
AND MERGED IN STRENGTH A MORE COMPLETED WHOLE.
THE EYE OF MIND AND EYE OF SOUL IN TOUCH
ON A COMMON GROUND OF TRUTH.

                                        W. H. W.

WITH NATURE-WARP OF NAKED WEED BY PRINTER-CRAFT IMPRISONED, WE WEAVE THIS INTERLINEAR WEB. A RYTHMIC CHANGING PLAY OF ORDERED SPACE AND IMAGE SEEKING TRACE OUR FABRIC MAKES, TO CLOTHE WITH CHASTITY AND GRACE OUR AUTHOR'S GENTLE WORD. APPRECIATION OF THE BEAUTY IN HIS WORK WE WEAVE, —IN PART OURSELVES TO PLEASE, YET MAY WE BETTER FARE, AND, WEAVING SO, WITH YOU OUR PLEASURE SHARE.

F. L. W.

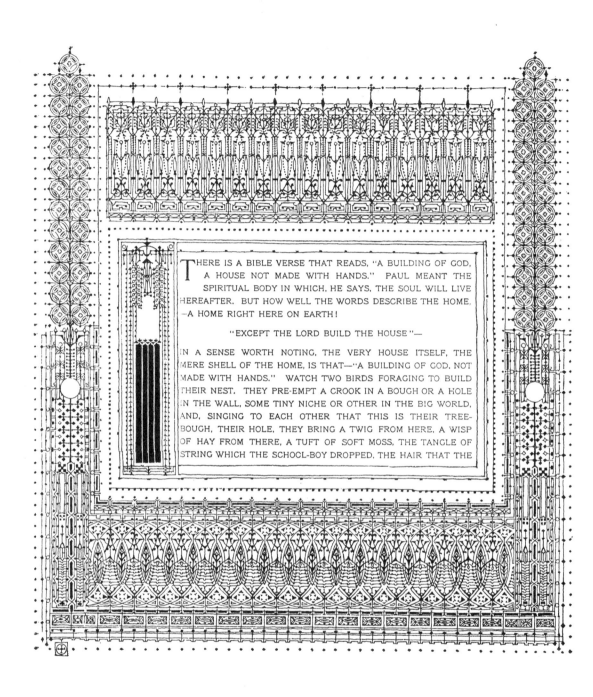

THERE IS A BIBLE VERSE THAT READS, "A BUILDING OF GOD, A HOUSE NOT MADE WITH HANDS." PAUL MEANT THE SPIRITUAL BODY IN WHICH, HE SAYS, THE SOUL WILL LIVE HEREAFTER. BUT HOW WELL THE WORDS DESCRIBE THE HOME, —A HOME RIGHT HERE ON EARTH!

"EXCEPT THE LORD BUILD THE HOUSE"—

IN A SENSE WORTH NOTING, THE VERY HOUSE ITSELF, THE MERE SHELL OF THE HOME, IS THAT—"A BUILDING OF GOD, NOT MADE WITH HANDS." WATCH TWO BIRDS FORAGING TO BUILD THEIR NEST. THEY PRE-EMPT A CROOK IN A BOUGH OR A HOLE IN THE WALL, SOME TINY NICHE OR OTHER IN THE BIG WORLD, AND, SINGING TO EACH OTHER THAT THIS IS THEIR TREE-BOUGH, THEIR HOLE, THEY BRING A TWIG FROM HERE, A WISP OF HAY FROM THERE, A TUFT OF SOFT MOSS, THE TANGLE OF STRING WHICH THE SCHOOL-BOY DROPPED, THE HAIR THAT THE

THE HOUSE BEAUTIFUL
CHAPTER ONE
THE BUILDING OF THE HOUSE."

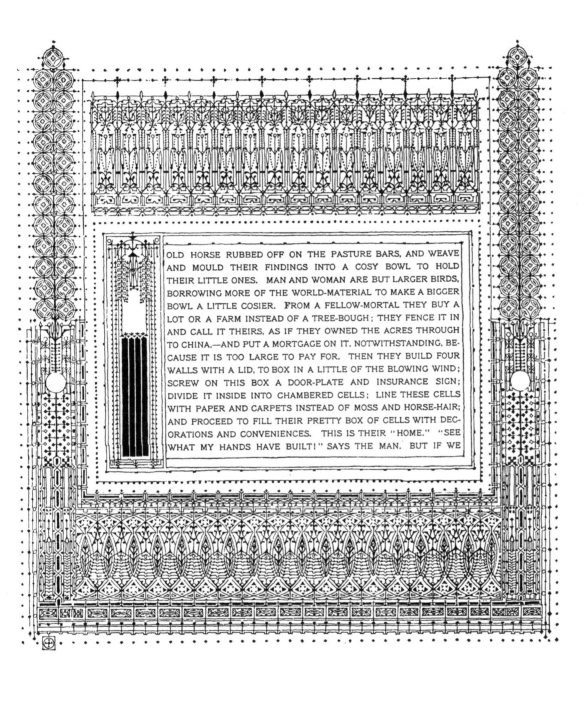

OLD HORSE RUBBED OFF ON THE PASTURE BARS, AND WEAVE AND MOULD THEIR FINDINGS INTO A COSY BOWL TO HOLD THEIR LITTLE ONES. MAN AND WOMAN ARE BUT LARGER BIRDS, BORROWING MORE OF THE WORLD-MATERIAL TO MAKE A BIGGER BOWL A LITTLE COSIER. FROM A FELLOW-MORTAL THEY BUY A LOT OR A FARM INSTEAD OF A TREE-BOUGH; THEY FENCE IT IN AND CALL IT THEIRS, AS IF THEY OWNED THE ACRES THROUGH TO CHINA,—AND PUT A MORTGAGE ON IT, NOTWITHSTANDING, BE-CAUSE IT IS TOO LARGE TO PAY FOR. THEN THEY BUILD FOUR WALLS WITH A LID, TO BOX IN A LITTLE OF THE BLOWING WIND; SCREW ON THIS BOX A DOOR-PLATE AND INSURANCE SIGN; DIVIDE IT INSIDE INTO CHAMBERED CELLS; LINE THESE CELLS WITH PAPER AND CARPETS INSTEAD OF MOSS AND HORSE-HAIR; AND PROCEED TO FILL THEIR PRETTY BOX OF CELLS WITH DEC-ORATIONS AND CONVENIENCES. THIS IS THEIR "HOME." "SEE WHAT MY HANDS HAVE BUILT!" SAYS THE MAN. BUT IF WE

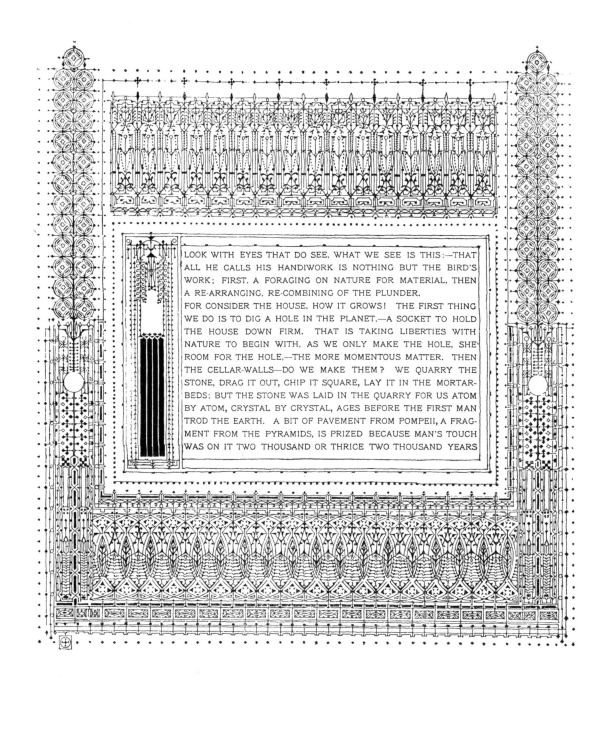

LOOK WITH EYES THAT DO SEE, WHAT WE SEE IS THIS:—THAT ALL HE CALLS HIS HANDIWORK IS NOTHING BUT THE BIRD'S WORK; FIRST, A FORAGING ON NATURE FOR MATERIAL, THEN A RE-ARRANGING, RE-COMBINING OF THE PLUNDER.

FOR CONSIDER THE HOUSE, HOW IT GROWS! THE FIRST THING WE DO IS TO DIG A HOLE IN THE PLANET,—A SOCKET TO HOLD THE HOUSE DOWN FIRM. THAT IS TAKING LIBERTIES WITH NATURE TO BEGIN WITH, AS WE ONLY MAKE THE HOLE, SHE ROOM FOR THE HOLE,—THE MORE MOMENTOUS MATTER. THEN THE CELLAR-WALLS—DO WE MAKE THEM? WE QUARRY THE STONE, DRAG IT OUT, CHIP IT SQUARE, LAY IT IN THE MORTAR-BEDS; BUT THE STONE WAS LAID IN THE QUARRY FOR US ATOM BY ATOM, CRYSTAL BY CRYSTAL, AGES BEFORE THE FIRST MAN TROD THE EARTH. A BIT OF PAVEMENT FROM POMPEII, A FRAG-MENT FROM THE PYRAMIDS, IS PRIZED BECAUSE MAN'S TOUCH WAS ON IT TWO THOUSAND OR THRICE TWO THOUSAND YEARS

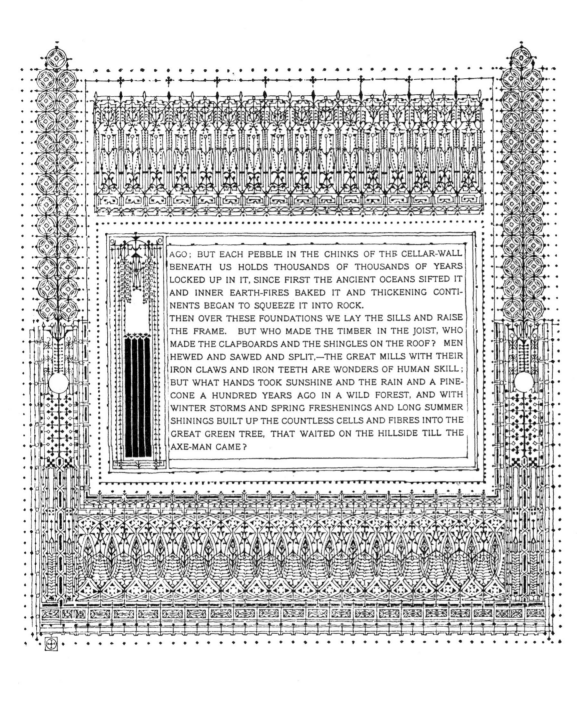

AGO; BUT EACH PEBBLE IN THE CHINKS OF THE CELLAR-WALL
BENEATH US HOLDS THOUSANDS OF THOUSANDS OF YEARS
LOCKED UP IN IT, SINCE FIRST THE ANCIENT OCEANS SIFTED IT
AND INNER EARTH-FIRES BAKED IT AND THICKENING CONTI-
NENTS BEGAN TO SQUEEZE IT INTO ROCK.

THEN OVER THESE FOUNDATIONS WE LAY THE SILLS AND RAISE
THE FRAME. BUT WHO MADE THE TIMBER IN THE JOIST, WHO
MADE THE CLAPBOARDS AND THE SHINGLES ON THE ROOF? MEN
HEWED AND SAWED AND SPLIT,—THE GREAT MILLS WITH THEIR
IRON CLAWS AND IRON TEETH ARE WONDERS OF HUMAN SKILL;
BUT WHAT HANDS TOOK SUNSHINE AND THE RAIN AND A PINE-
CONE A HUNDRED YEARS AGO IN A WILD FOREST, AND WITH
WINTER STORMS AND SPRING FRESHENINGS AND LONG SUMMER
SHININGS BUILT UP THE COUNTLESS CELLS AND FIBRES INTO THE
GREAT GREEN TREE, THAT WAITED ON THE HILLSIDE TILL THE
AXE-MAN CAME?

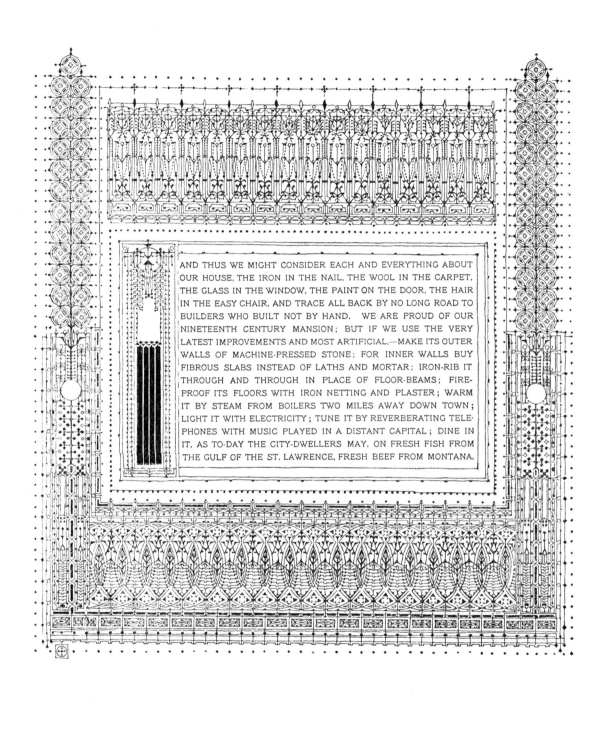

AND THUS WE MIGHT CONSIDER EACH AND EVERYTHING ABOUT OUR HOUSE, THE IRON IN THE NAIL, THE WOOL IN THE CARPET, THE GLASS IN THE WINDOW, THE PAINT ON THE DOOR, THE HAIR IN THE EASY CHAIR, AND TRACE ALL BACK BY NO LONG ROAD TO BUILDERS WHO BUILT NOT BY HAND. WE ARE PROUD OF OUR NINETEENTH CENTURY MANSION; BUT IF WE USE THE VERY LATEST IMPROVEMENTS AND MOST ARTIFICIAL,—MAKE ITS OUTER WALLS OF MACHINE-PRESSED STONE; FOR INNER WALLS BUY FIBROUS SLABS INSTEAD OF LATHS AND MORTAR; IRON-RIB IT THROUGH AND THROUGH IN PLACE OF FLOOR-BEAMS; FIRE-PROOF ITS FLOORS WITH IRON NETTING AND PLASTER; WARM IT BY STEAM FROM BOILERS TWO MILES AWAY DOWN TOWN; LIGHT IT WITH ELECTRICITY; TUNE IT BY REVERBERATING TELE-PHONES WITH MUSIC PLAYED IN A DISTANT CAPITAL; DINE IN IT, AS TO-DAY THE CITY-DWELLERS MAY, ON FRESH FISH FROM THE GULF OF THE ST. LAWRENCE, FRESH BEEF FROM MONTANA,

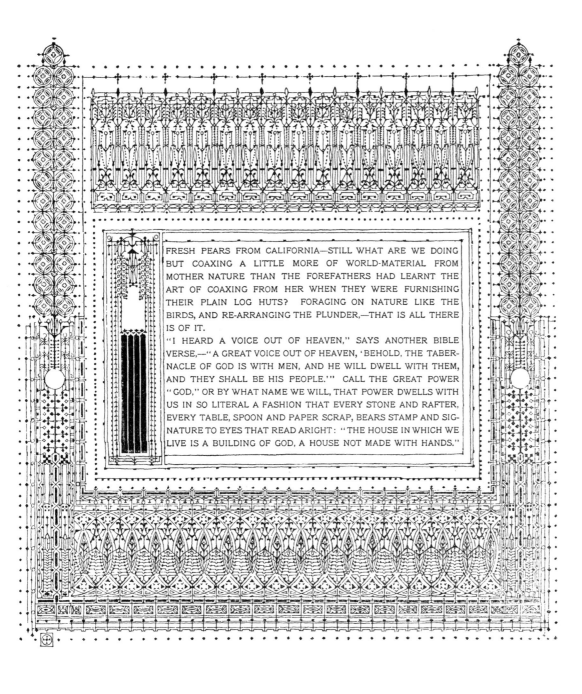

FRESH PEARS FROM CALIFORNIA—STILL WHAT ARE WE DOING BUT COAXING A LITTLE MORE OF WORLD-MATERIAL FROM MOTHER NATURE THAN THE FOREFATHERS HAD LEARNT THE ART OF COAXING FROM HER WHEN THEY WERE FURNISHING THEIR PLAIN LOG HUTS? FORAGING ON NATURE LIKE THE BIRDS, AND RE-ARRANGING THE PLUNDER,—THAT IS ALL THERE IS OF IT.

"I HEARD A VOICE OUT OF HEAVEN," SAYS ANOTHER BIBLE VERSE,—"A GREAT VOICE OUT OF HEAVEN, 'BEHOLD, THE TABERNACLE OF GOD IS WITH MEN, AND HE WILL DWELL WITH THEM, AND THEY SHALL BE HIS PEOPLE.'" CALL THE GREAT POWER "GOD," OR BY WHAT NAME WE WILL, THAT POWER DWELLS WITH US IN SO LITERAL A FASHION THAT EVERY STONE AND RAFTER, EVERY TABLE, SPOON AND PAPER SCRAP, BEARS STAMP AND SIGNATURE TO EYES THAT READ ARIGHT: "THE HOUSE IN WHICH WE LIVE IS A BUILDING OF GOD, A HOUSE NOT MADE WITH HANDS."

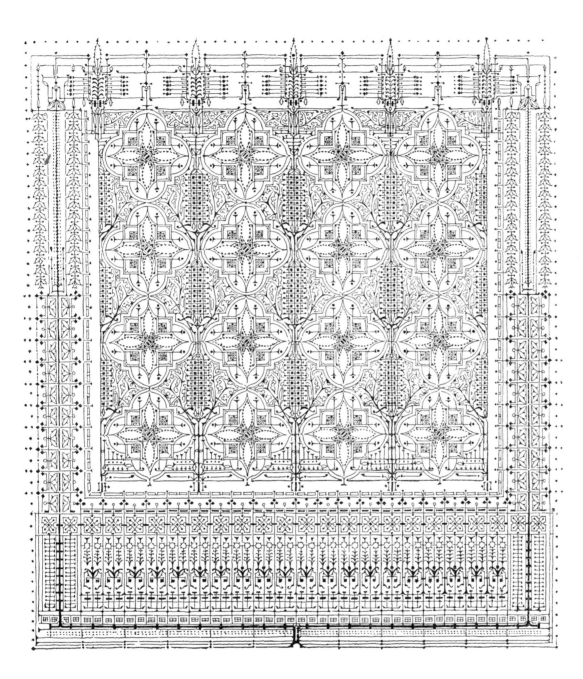

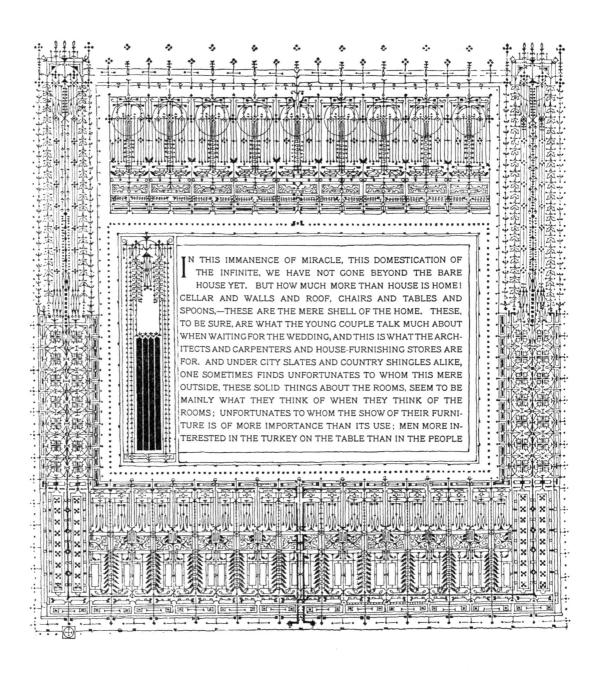

IN THIS IMMANENCE OF MIRACLE, THIS DOMESTICATION OF THE INFINITE, WE HAVE NOT GONE BEYOND THE BARE HOUSE YET. BUT HOW MUCH MORE THAN HOUSE IS HOME! CELLAR AND WALLS AND ROOF, CHAIRS AND TABLES AND SPOONS,—THESE ARE THE MERE SHELL OF THE HOME. THESE, TO BE SURE, ARE WHAT THE YOUNG COUPLE TALK MUCH ABOUT WHEN WAITING FOR THE WEDDING, AND THIS IS WHAT THE ARCH-ITECTS AND CARPENTERS AND HOUSE-FURNISHING STORES ARE FOR. AND UNDER CITY SLATES AND COUNTRY SHINGLES ALIKE, ONE SOMETIMES FINDS UNFORTUNATES TO WHOM THIS MERE OUTSIDE, THESE SOLID THINGS ABOUT THE ROOMS, SEEM TO BE MAINLY WHAT THEY THINK OF WHEN THEY THINK OF THE ROOMS; UNFORTUNATES TO WHOM THE SHOW OF THEIR FURNI-TURE IS OF MORE IMPORTANCE THAN ITS USE; MEN MORE IN-TERESTED IN THE TURKEY ON THE TABLE THAN IN THE PEOPLE

THE HOUSE BEAUTIFUL
CHAPTER TWO
HOUSE FURNISHING."

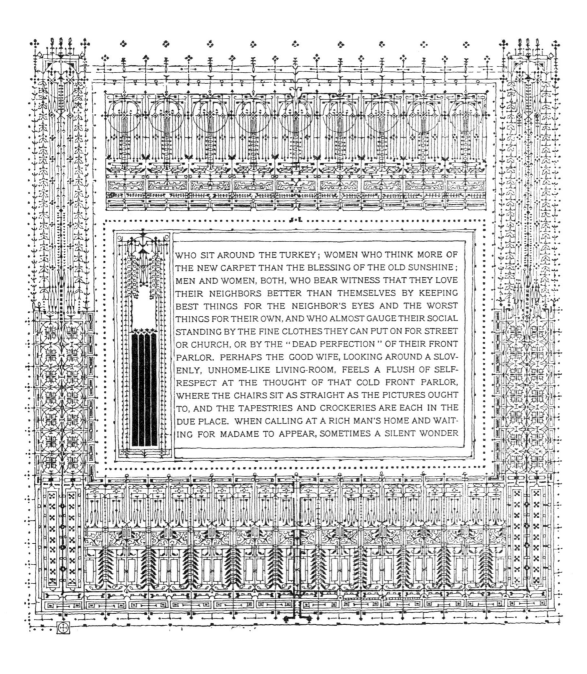

WHO SIT AROUND THE TURKEY; WOMEN WHO THINK MORE OF THE NEW CARPET THAN THE BLESSING OF THE OLD SUNSHINE; MEN AND WOMEN, BOTH, WHO BEAR WITNESS THAT THEY LOVE THEIR NEIGHBORS BETTER THAN THEMSELVES BY KEEPING BEST THINGS FOR THE NEIGHBOR'S EYES AND THE WORST THINGS FOR THEIR OWN, AND WHO ALMOST GAUGE THEIR SOCIAL STANDING BY THE FINE CLOTHES THEY CAN PUT ON FOR STREET OR CHURCH, OR BY THE "DEAD PERFECTION" OF THEIR FRONT PARLOR. PERHAPS THE GOOD WIFE, LOOKING AROUND A SLOVENLY, UNHOME-LIKE LIVING-ROOM, FEELS A FLUSH OF SELF-RESPECT AT THE THOUGHT OF THAT COLD FRONT PARLOR, WHERE THE CHAIRS SIT AS STRAIGHT AS THE PICTURES OUGHT TO, AND THE TAPESTRIES AND CROCKERIES ARE EACH IN THE DUE PLACE. WHEN CALLING AT A RICH MAN'S HOME AND WAITING FOR MADAME TO APPEAR, SOMETIMES A SILENT WONDER

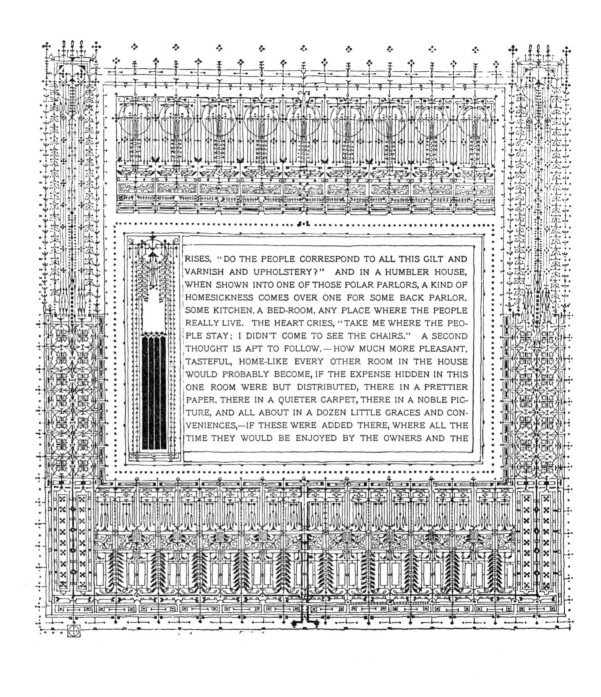

RISES, "DO THE PEOPLE CORRESPOND TO ALL THIS GILT AND VARNISH AND UPHOLSTERY?" AND IN A HUMBLER HOUSE, WHEN SHOWN INTO ONE OF THOSE POLAR PARLORS, A KIND OF HOMESICKNESS COMES OVER ONE FOR SOME BACK PARLOR, SOME KITCHEN, A BED-ROOM, ANY PLACE WHERE THE PEOPLE REALLY LIVE. THE HEART CRIES, "TAKE ME WHERE THE PEO-PLE STAY; I DIDN'T COME TO SEE THE CHAIRS." A SECOND THOUGHT IS APT TO FOLLOW, — HOW MUCH MORE PLEASANT, TASTEFUL, HOME-LIKE EVERY OTHER ROOM IN THE HOUSE WOULD PROBABLY BECOME, IF THE EXPENSE HIDDEN IN THIS ONE ROOM WERE BUT DISTRIBUTED, THERE IN A PRETTIER PAPER, THERE IN A QUIETER CARPET, THERE IN A NOBLE PIC-TURE, AND ALL ABOUT IN A DOZEN LITTLE GRACES AND CON-VENIENCES,—IF THESE WERE ADDED THERE, WHERE ALL THE TIME THEY WOULD BE ENJOYED BY THE OWNERS AND THE

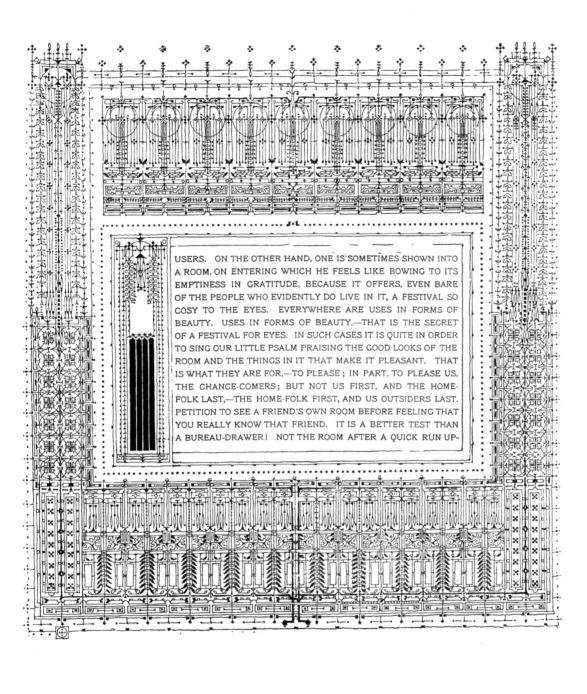

USERS. ON THE OTHER HAND, ONE IS SOMETIMES SHOWN INTO A ROOM, ON ENTERING WHICH HE FEELS LIKE BOWING TO ITS EMPTINESS IN GRATITUDE, BECAUSE IT OFFERS, EVEN BARE OF THE PEOPLE WHO EVIDENTLY DO LIVE IN IT, A FESTIVAL SO COSY TO THE EYES. EVERYWHERE ARE USES IN FORMS OF BEAUTY. USES IN FORMS OF BEAUTY,—THAT IS THE SECRET OF A FESTIVAL FOR EYES. IN SUCH CASES IT IS QUITE IN ORDER TO SING OUR LITTLE PSALM PRAISING THE GOOD LOOKS OF THE ROOM AND THE THINGS IN IT THAT MAKE IT PLEASANT. THAT IS WHAT THEY ARE FOR,—TO PLEASE ; IN PART, TO PLEASE US, THE CHANCE-COMERS; BUT NOT US FIRST, AND THE HOME-FOLK LAST,—THE HOME-FOLK FIRST, AND US OUTSIDERS LAST. PETITION TO SEE A FRIEND'S OWN ROOM BEFORE FEELING THAT YOU REALLY KNOW THAT FRIEND. IT IS A BETTER TEST THAN A BUREAU-DRAWER! NOT THE ROOM AFTER A QUICK RUN UP-

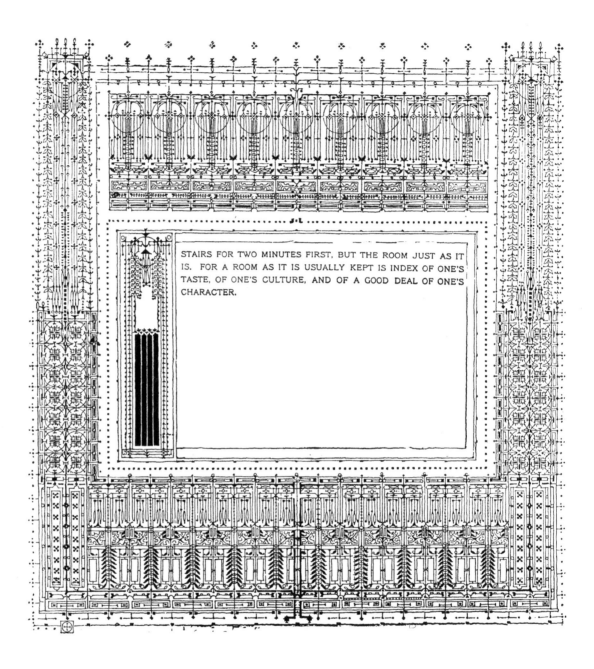

STAIRS FOR TWO MINUTES FIRST, BUT THE ROOM JUST AS IT IS. FOR A ROOM AS IT IS USUALLY KEPT IS INDEX OF ONE'S TASTE, OF ONE'S CULTURE, AND OF A GOOD DEAL OF ONE'S CHARACTER.

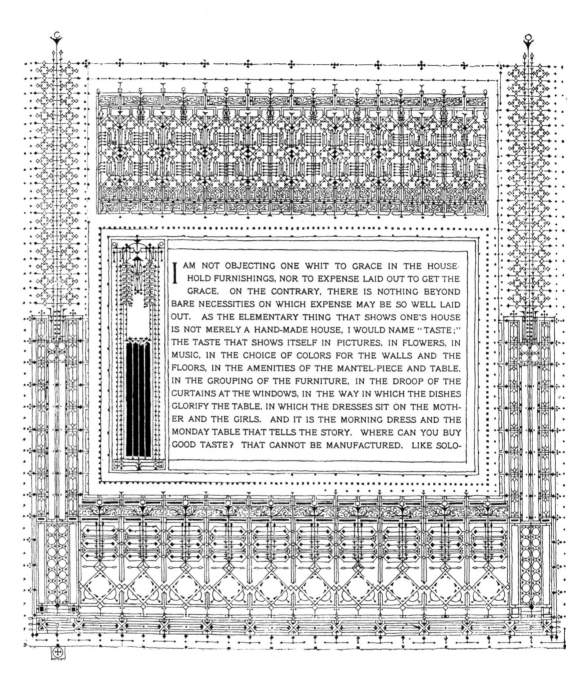

I AM NOT OBJECTING ONE WHIT TO GRACE IN THE HOUSE-HOLD FURNISHINGS, NOR TO EXPENSE LAID OUT TO GET THE GRACE. ON THE CONTRARY, THERE IS NOTHING BEYOND BARE NECESSITIES ON WHICH EXPENSE MAY BE SO WELL LAID OUT. AS THE ELEMENTARY THING THAT SHOWS ONE'S HOUSE IS NOT MERELY A HAND-MADE HOUSE, I WOULD NAME "TASTE;" THE TASTE THAT SHOWS ITSELF IN PICTURES, IN FLOWERS, IN MUSIC, IN THE CHOICE OF COLORS FOR THE WALLS AND THE FLOORS, IN THE AMENITIES OF THE MANTEL-PIECE AND TABLE, IN THE GROUPING OF THE FURNITURE, IN THE DROOP OF THE CURTAINS AT THE WINDOWS, IN THE WAY IN WHICH THE DISHES GLORIFY THE TABLE, IN WHICH THE DRESSES SIT ON THE MOTH-ER AND THE GIRLS. AND IT IS THE MORNING DRESS AND THE MONDAY TABLE THAT TELLS THE STORY. WHERE CAN YOU BUY GOOD TASTE? THAT CANNOT BE MANUFACTURED. LIKE SOLO-

THE HOUSE BEAUTIFUL
CHAPTER THREE
THE IDEAL OF BEAUTY."

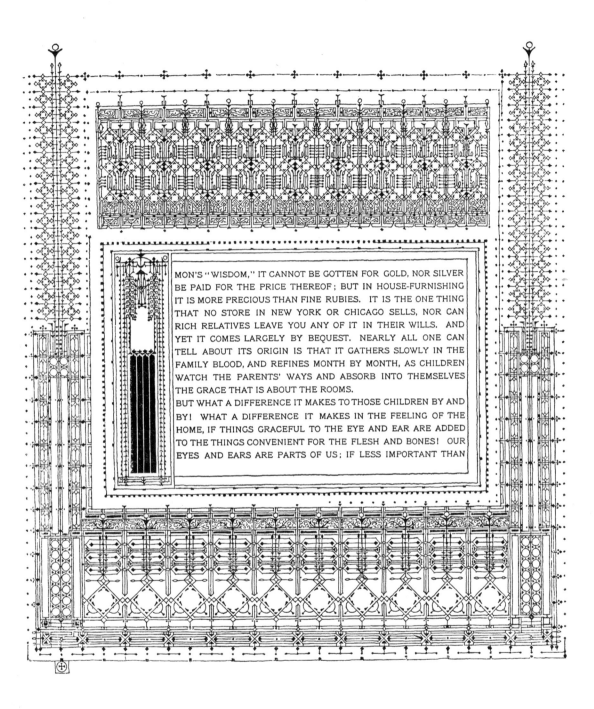

MON'S "WISDOM," IT CANNOT BE GOTTEN FOR GOLD, NOR SILVER BE PAID FOR THE PRICE THEREOF; BUT IN HOUSE-FURNISHING IT IS MORE PRECIOUS THAN FINE RUBIES. IT IS THE ONE THING THAT NO STORE IN NEW YORK OR CHICAGO SELLS, NOR CAN RICH RELATIVES LEAVE YOU ANY OF IT IN THEIR WILLS. AND YET IT COMES LARGELY BY BEQUEST. NEARLY ALL ONE CAN TELL ABOUT ITS ORIGIN IS THAT IT GATHERS SLOWLY IN THE FAMILY BLOOD, AND REFINES MONTH BY MONTH, AS CHILDREN WATCH THE PARENTS' WAYS AND ABSORB INTO THEMSELVES THE GRACE THAT IS ABOUT THE ROOMS.

BUT WHAT A DIFFERENCE IT MAKES TO THOSE CHILDREN BY AND BY! WHAT A DIFFERENCE IT MAKES IN THE FEELING OF THE HOME, IF THINGS GRACEFUL TO THE EYE AND EAR ARE ADDED TO THE THINGS CONVENIENT FOR THE FLESH AND BONES! OUR EYES AND EARS ARE PARTS OF US; IF LESS IMPORTANT THAN

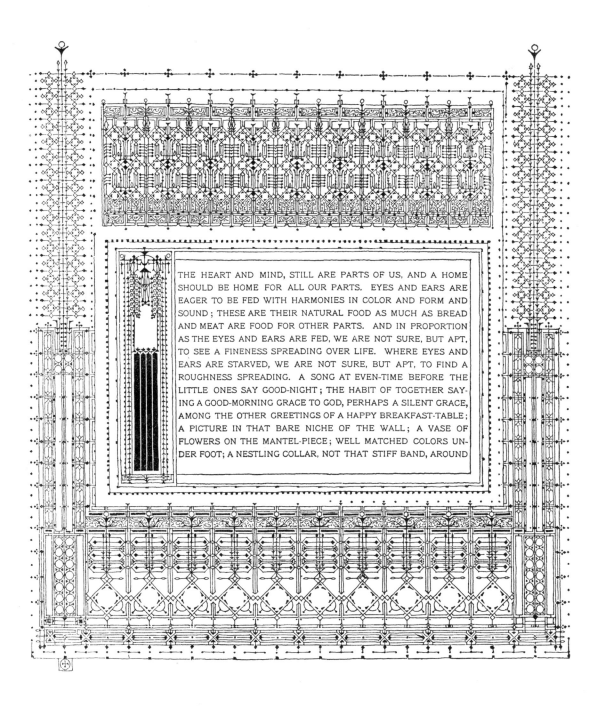

THE HEART AND MIND, STILL ARE PARTS OF US, AND A HOME
SHOULD BE HOME FOR ALL OUR PARTS. EYES AND EARS ARE
EAGER TO BE FED WITH HARMONIES IN COLOR AND FORM AND
SOUND ; THESE ARE THEIR NATURAL FOOD AS MUCH AS BREAD
AND MEAT ARE FOOD FOR OTHER PARTS. AND IN PROPORTION
AS THE EYES AND EARS ARE FED, WE ARE NOT SURE, BUT APT,
TO SEE A FINENESS SPREADING OVER LIFE. WHERE EYES AND
EARS ARE STARVED, WE ARE NOT SURE, BUT APT, TO FIND A
ROUGHNESS SPREADING. A SONG AT EVEN-TIME BEFORE THE
LITTLE ONES SAY GOOD-NIGHT ; THE HABIT OF TOGETHER SAY-
ING A GOOD-MORNING GRACE TO GOD, PERHAPS A SILENT GRACE,
AMONG THE OTHER GREETINGS OF A HAPPY BREAKFAST-TABLE ;
A PICTURE IN THAT BARE NICHE OF THE WALL ; A VASE OF
FLOWERS ON THE MANTEL-PIECE ; WELL MATCHED COLORS UN-
DER FOOT ; A NESTLING COLLAR, NOT THAT STIFF BAND, AROUND

THE NECK; BRUSHED BOOTS, IF BOOTS IT MUST BE, WHEN THE
FAMILY ARE ALL TOGETHER; THE TEA-TABLE TASTEFULLY, HOW-
EVER SIMPLY, SET, INSTEAD OF DISHES IN A HUDDLE,—THESE
ALL ARE LITTLE THINGS; YOU WOULD HARDLY NOTICE THEM AS
SINGLE THINGS; YOU WOULD NOT CALL THEM " RELIGION," THEY
ARE NOT " MORALS," THEY SCARCELY EVEN CLASS UNDER THE
HEAD OF " MANNERS."   MEN AND WOMEN CAN BE GOOD PARENTS
AND VALUABLE CITIZENS WITHOUT THEM.   AND YET, AND YET,
ONE CANNOT FORGET THAT, AS THE YEARS RUN ON, THESE
TRIFLES OF THE HOME WILL MAKE NO LITTLE OF THE DIFFER-
ENCE BETWEEN COARSE GRAIN AND FINE GRAIN IN US AND IN
OUR CHILDREN, WHEN THEY GROW UP.

BESIDES, THIS TASTE FOR GRACE IS NOTHING HARD TO GRATIFY
IN THESE DAYS. IT IS MUCH HARDER TO GET THE GOOD TASTE
THAN THE MEANS BY WHICH TO GRATIFY IT. NOT SPLENDOR,

BUT HARMONY, IS GRACE; NOT MANY THINGS, BUT PICTURESQUE THINGS. THE IDEALS OF BEAUTY ARE FOUND IN SIMPLE, REST-FUL THINGS FAR OFTENER THAN IN ORNATE THINGS. OF TWO GIVEN FORMS FOR THE SAME ARTICLE—A CHAIR, A TABLE, A DRESS—THE FORM THAT IS LEAST ORNATE IS COMMONLY THE MORE USEFUL, AND THIS MORE USEFUL FORM WILL COMMONLY BY ARTIST EYES BE FOUND THE HANDSOMER. A MAN IN HIS WORKING CLOTHES IS USUALLY MORE PICTURESQUE THAN THAT SAME MAN IN HIS SUNDAY CLOTHES; THE LIVING-ROOM MORE PICTURESQUE THAN THE PARLOR. "AVOID THE SUPERFLUOUS," IS A RECIPE THAT OF ITSELF WOULD CLEAR OUR ROOMS OF MUCH UNHANDSOME HANDSOMENESS. SCRATCH OUT THE "VERYS" FROM YOUR TALK, FROM YOUR WRITING, FROM YOUR HOUSE-FURNISHING.

A CERTAIN SENTENCE, ONLY EIGHT WORDS LONG, DID ME GREAT

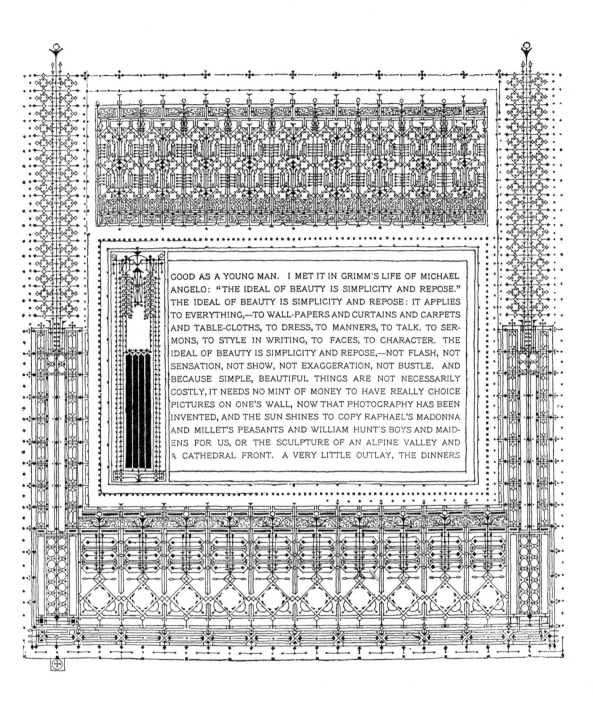

GOOD AS A YOUNG MAN. I MET IT IN GRIMM'S LIFE OF MICHAEL ANGELO: "THE IDEAL OF BEAUTY IS SIMPLICITY AND REPOSE." THE IDEAL OF BEAUTY IS SIMPLICITY AND REPOSE: IT APPLIES TO EVERYTHING,—TO WALL-PAPERS AND CURTAINS AND CARPETS AND TABLE-CLOTHS, TO DRESS, TO MANNERS, TO TALK, TO SERMONS, TO STYLE IN WRITING, TO FACES, TO CHARACTER. THE IDEAL OF BEAUTY IS SIMPLICITY AND REPOSE,—NOT FLASH, NOT SENSATION, NOT SHOW, NOT EXAGGERATION, NOT BUSTLE. AND BECAUSE SIMPLE, BEAUTIFUL THINGS ARE NOT NECESSARILY COSTLY, IT NEEDS NO MINT OF MONEY TO HAVE REALLY CHOICE PICTURES ON ONE'S WALL, NOW THAT PHOTOGRAPHY HAS BEEN INVENTED, AND THE SUN SHINES TO COPY RAPHAEL'S MADONNA AND MILLET'S PEASANTS AND WILLIAM HUNT'S BOYS AND MAIDENS FOR US, OR THE SCULPTURE OF AN ALPINE VALLEY AND A CATHEDRAL FRONT. A VERY LITTLE OUTLAY, THE DINNERS

CHEAPENED FOR A MONTH, WILL MAKE THE BARE DINING-ROOM
SO BEAUTIFUL THAT PLAIN DINNERS EVER AFTERWARDS TASTE
BETTER IN IT; IT REALLY IS ECONOMY AND SAVES A COURSE.

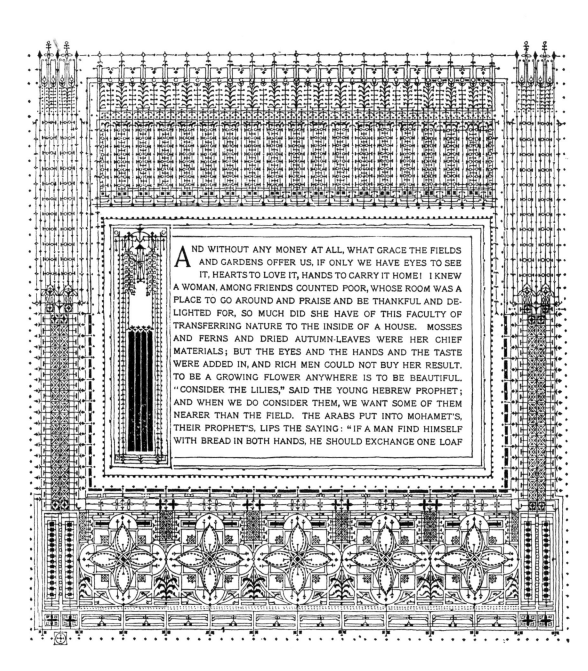

AND WITHOUT ANY MONEY AT ALL, WHAT GRACE THE FIELDS
AND GARDENS OFFER US, IF ONLY WE HAVE EYES TO SEE
IT, HEARTS TO LOVE IT, HANDS TO CARRY IT HOME! I KNEW
A WOMAN, AMONG FRIENDS COUNTED POOR, WHOSE ROOM WAS A
PLACE TO GO AROUND AND PRAISE AND BE THANKFUL AND DE-
LIGHTED FOR, SO MUCH DID SHE HAVE OF THIS FACULTY OF
TRANSFERRING NATURE TO THE INSIDE OF A HOUSE. MOSSES
AND FERNS AND DRIED AUTUMN-LEAVES WERE HER CHIEF
MATERIALS; BUT THE EYES AND THE HANDS AND THE TASTE
WERE ADDED IN, AND RICH MEN COULD NOT BUY HER RESULT.
TO BE A GROWING FLOWER ANYWHERE IS TO BE BEAUTIFUL.
"CONSIDER THE LILIES," SAID THE YOUNG HEBREW PROPHET;
AND WHEN WE DO CONSIDER THEM, WE WANT SOME OF THEM
NEARER THAN THE FIELD. THE ARABS PUT INTO MOHAMET'S,
THEIR PROPHET'S, LIPS THE SAYING: "IF A MAN FIND HIMSELF
WITH BREAD IN BOTH HANDS, HE SHOULD EXCHANGE ONE LOAF

THE HOUSE BEAUTIFUL
CHAPTER FOUR
FLOWER FURNITURE."

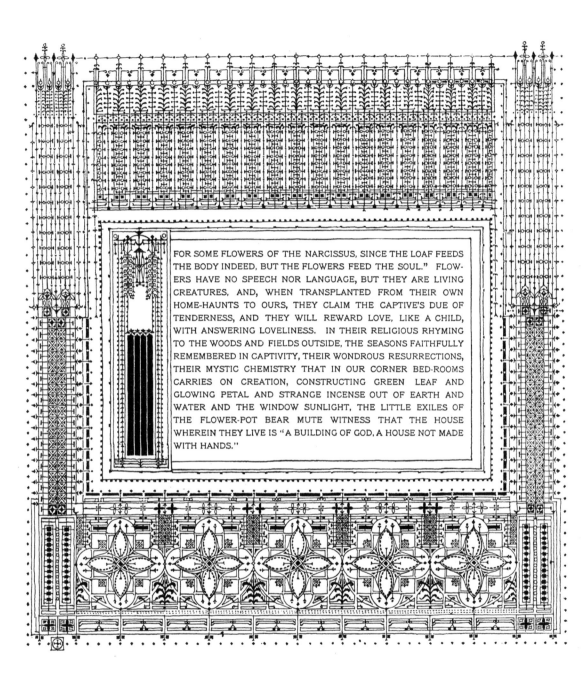

FOR SOME FLOWERS OF THE NARCISSUS, SINCE THE LOAF FEEDS THE BODY INDEED, BUT THE FLOWERS FEED THE SOUL." FLOWERS HAVE NO SPEECH NOR LANGUAGE, BUT THEY ARE LIVING CREATURES, AND, WHEN TRANSPLANTED FROM THEIR OWN HOME-HAUNTS TO OURS, THEY CLAIM THE CAPTIVE'S DUE OF TENDERNESS, AND THEY WILL REWARD LOVE, LIKE A CHILD, WITH ANSWERING LOVELINESS. IN THEIR RELIGIOUS RHYMING TO THE WOODS AND FIELDS OUTSIDE, THE SEASONS FAITHFULLY REMEMBERED IN CAPTIVITY, THEIR WONDROUS RESURRECTIONS, THEIR MYSTIC CHEMISTRY THAT IN OUR CORNER BED-ROOMS CARRIES ON CREATION, CONSTRUCTING GREEN LEAF AND GLOWING PETAL AND STRANGE INCENSE OUT OF EARTH AND WATER AND THE WINDOW SUNLIGHT, THE LITTLE EXILES OF THE FLOWER-POT BEAR MUTE WITNESS THAT THE HOUSE WHEREIN THEY LIVE IS "A BUILDING OF GOD, A HOUSE NOT MADE WITH HANDS."

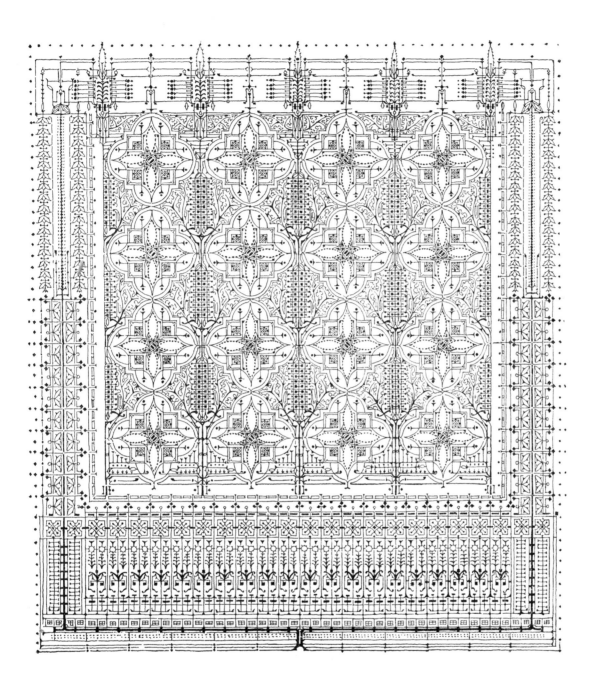

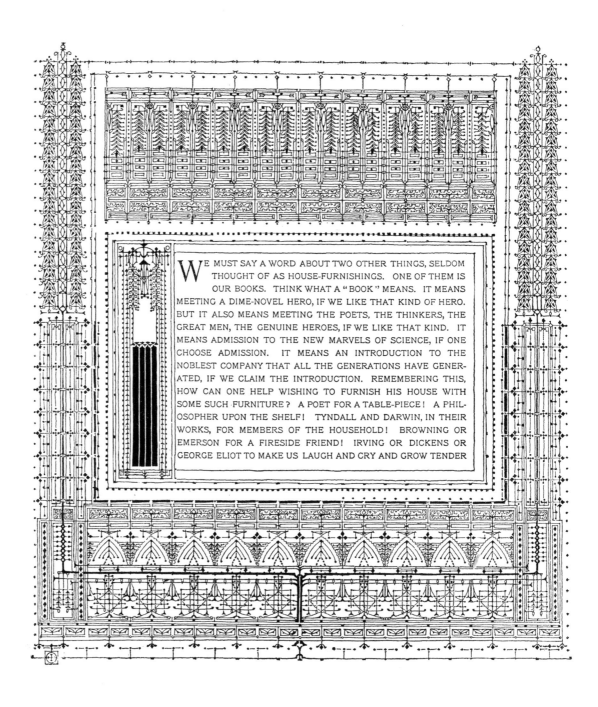

WE MUST SAY A WORD ABOUT TWO OTHER THINGS, SELDOM THOUGHT OF AS HOUSE-FURNISHINGS. ONE OF THEM IS OUR BOOKS. THINK WHAT A "BOOK" MEANS. IT MEANS MEETING A DIME-NOVEL HERO, IF WE LIKE THAT KIND OF HERO. BUT IT ALSO MEANS MEETING THE POETS, THE THINKERS, THE GREAT MEN, THE GENUINE HEROES, IF WE LIKE THAT KIND. IT MEANS ADMISSION TO THE NEW MARVELS OF SCIENCE, IF ONE CHOOSE ADMISSION. IT MEANS AN INTRODUCTION TO THE NOBLEST COMPANY THAT ALL THE GENERATIONS HAVE GENERATED, IF WE CLAIM THE INTRODUCTION. REMEMBERING THIS, HOW CAN ONE HELP WISHING TO FURNISH HIS HOUSE WITH SOME SUCH FURNITURE? A POET FOR A TABLE-PIECE! A PHILOSOPHER UPON THE SHELF! TYNDALL AND DARWIN, IN THEIR WORKS, FOR MEMBERS OF THE HOUSEHOLD! BROWNING OR EMERSON FOR A FIRESIDE FRIEND! IRVING OR DICKENS OR GEORGE ELIOT TO MAKE US LAUGH AND CRY AND GROW TENDER

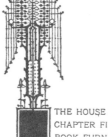

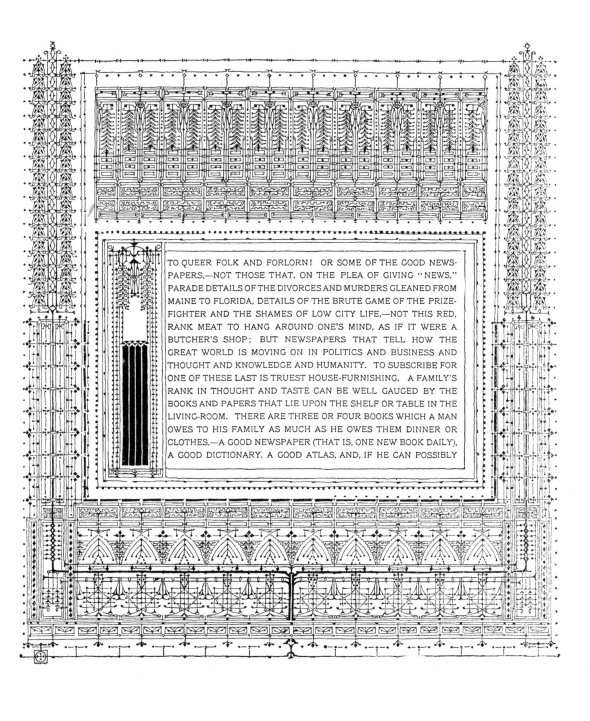

TO QUEER FOLK AND FORLORN! OR SOME OF THE GOOD NEWS-
PAPERS,—NOT THOSE THAT, ON THE PLEA OF GIVING "NEWS,"
PARADE DETAILS OF THE DIVORCES AND MURDERS GLEANED FROM
MAINE TO FLORIDA, DETAILS OF THE BRUTE GAME OF THE PRIZE-
FIGHTER AND THE SHAMES OF LOW CITY LIFE,—NOT THIS RED,
RANK MEAT TO HANG AROUND ONE'S MIND, AS IF IT WERE A
BUTCHER'S SHOP; BUT NEWSPAPERS THAT TELL HOW THE
GREAT WORLD IS MOVING ON IN POLITICS AND BUSINESS AND
THOUGHT AND KNOWLEDGE AND HUMANITY. TO SUBSCRIBE FOR
ONE OF THESE LAST IS TRUEST HOUSE-FURNISHING. A FAMILY'S
RANK IN THOUGHT AND TASTE CAN BE WELL GAUGED BY THE
BOOKS AND PAPERS THAT LIE UPON THE SHELF OR TABLE IN THE
LIVING-ROOM. THERE ARE THREE OR FOUR BOOKS WHICH A MAN
OWES TO HIS FAMILY AS MUCH AS HE OWES THEM DINNER OR
CLOTHES,—A GOOD NEWSPAPER (THAT IS, ONE NEW BOOK DAILY),
A GOOD DICTIONARY, A GOOD ATLAS, AND, IF HE CAN POSSIBLY

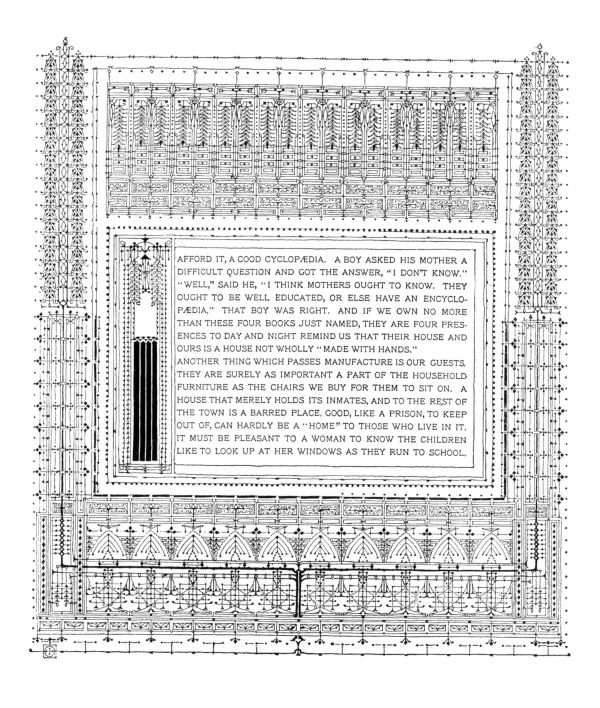

AFFORD IT, A GOOD CYCLOPÆDIA. A BOY ASKED HIS MOTHER A DIFFICULT QUESTION AND GOT THE ANSWER, "I DON'T KNOW." "WELL," SAID HE, "I THINK MOTHERS OUGHT TO KNOW. THEY OUGHT TO BE WELL EDUCATED, OR ELSE HAVE AN ENCYCLO-PÆDIA," THAT BOY WAS RIGHT. AND IF WE OWN NO MORE THAN THESE FOUR BOOKS JUST NAMED, THEY ARE FOUR PRES-ENCES TO DAY AND NIGHT REMIND US THAT THEIR HOUSE AND OURS IS A HOUSE NOT WHOLLY "MADE WITH HANDS."

ANOTHER THING WHICH PASSES MANUFACTURE IS OUR GUESTS. THEY ARE SURELY AS IMPORTANT A PART OF THE HOUSEHOLD FURNITURE AS THE CHAIRS WE BUY FOR THEM TO SIT ON. A HOUSE THAT MERELY HOLDS ITS INMATES, AND TO THE REST OF THE TOWN IS A BARRED PLACE, GOOD, LIKE A PRISON, TO KEEP OUT OF, CAN HARDLY BE A "HOME" TO THOSE WHO LIVE IN IT. IT MUST BE PLEASANT TO A WOMAN TO KNOW THE CHILDREN LIKE TO LOOK UP AT HER WINDOWS AS THEY RUN TO SCHOOL.

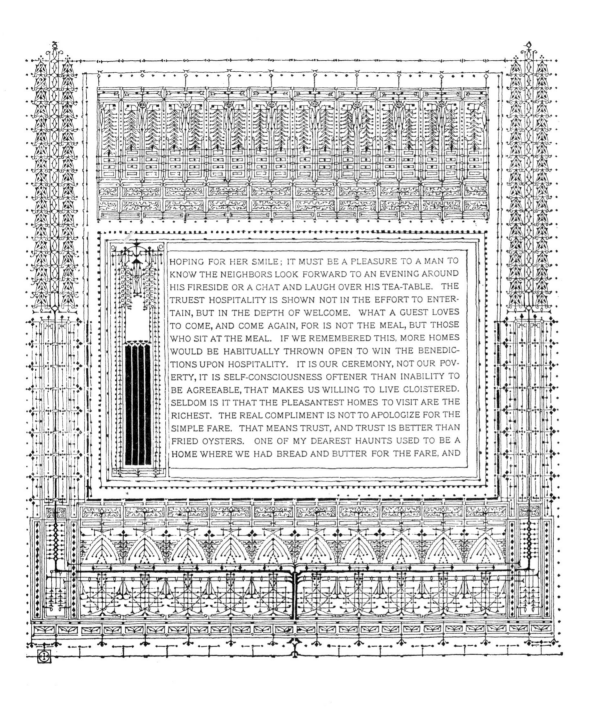

HOPING FOR HER SMILE; IT MUST BE A PLEASURE TO A MAN TO KNOW THE NEIGHBORS LOOK FORWARD TO AN EVENING AROUND HIS FIRESIDE OR A CHAT AND LAUGH OVER HIS TEA-TABLE. THE TRUEST HOSPITALITY IS SHOWN NOT IN THE EFFORT TO ENTERTAIN, BUT IN THE DEPTH OF WELCOME. WHAT A GUEST LOVES TO COME, AND COME AGAIN, FOR IS NOT THE MEAL, BUT THOSE WHO SIT AT THE MEAL. IF WE REMEMBERED THIS, MORE HOMES WOULD BE HABITUALLY THROWN OPEN TO WIN THE BENEDICTIONS UPON HOSPITALITY. IT IS OUR CEREMONY, NOT OUR POVERTY, IT IS SELF-CONSCIOUSNESS OFTENER THAN INABILITY TO BE AGREEABLE, THAT MAKES US WILLING TO LIVE CLOISTERED. SELDOM IS IT THAT THE PLEASANTEST HOMES TO VISIT ARE THE RICHEST. THE REAL COMPLIMENT IS NOT TO APOLOGIZE FOR THE SIMPLE FARE. THAT MEANS TRUST, AND TRUST IS BETTER THAN FRIED OYSTERS. ONE OF MY DEAREST HAUNTS USED TO BE A HOME WHERE WE HAD BREAD AND BUTTER FOR THE FARE, AND

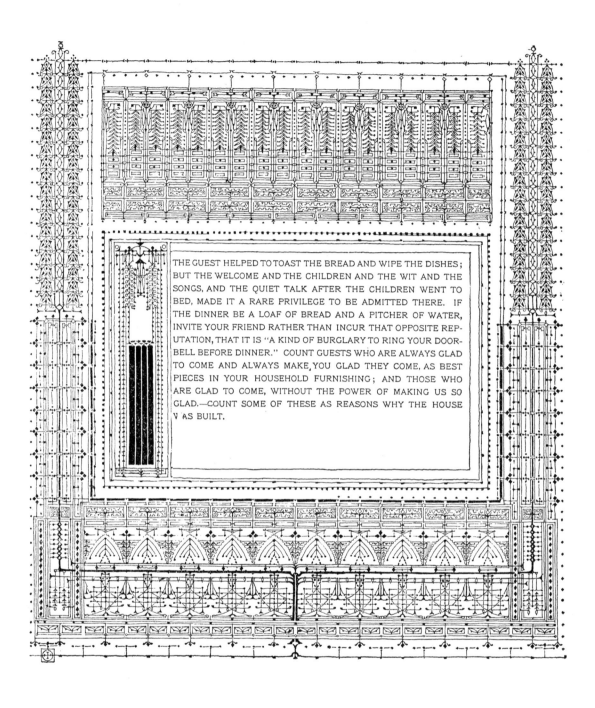

THE GUEST HELPED TO TOAST THE BREAD AND WIPE THE DISHES; BUT THE WELCOME AND THE CHILDREN AND THE WIT AND THE SONGS, AND THE QUIET TALK AFTER THE CHILDREN WENT TO BED, MADE IT A RARE PRIVILEGE TO BE ADMITTED THERE. IF THE DINNER BE A LOAF OF BREAD AND A PITCHER OF WATER, INVITE YOUR FRIEND RATHER THAN INCUR THAT OPPOSITE REPUTATION, THAT IT IS "A KIND OF BURGLARY TO RING YOUR DOORBELL BEFORE DINNER." COUNT GUESTS WHO ARE ALWAYS GLAD TO COME AND ALWAYS MAKE YOU GLAD THEY COME, AS BEST PIECES IN YOUR HOUSEHOLD FURNISHING; AND THOSE WHO ARE GLAD TO COME, WITHOUT THE POWER OF MAKING US SO GLAD.—COUNT SOME OF THESE AS REASONS WHY THE HOUSE WAS BUILT.

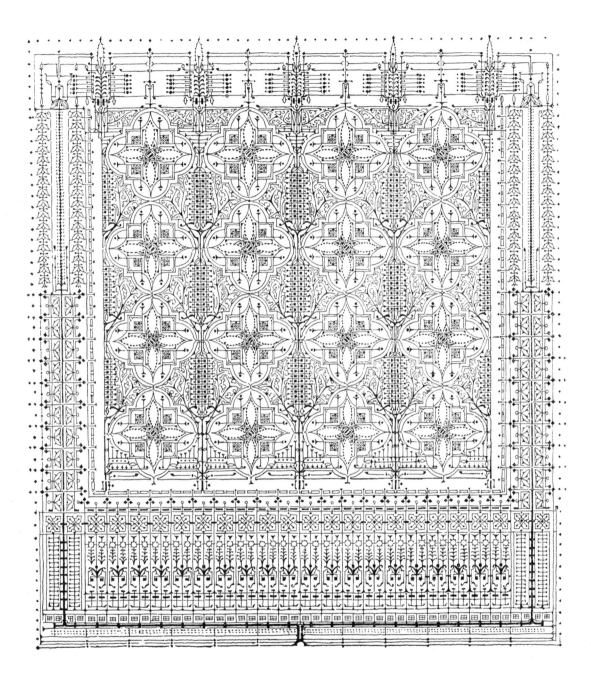

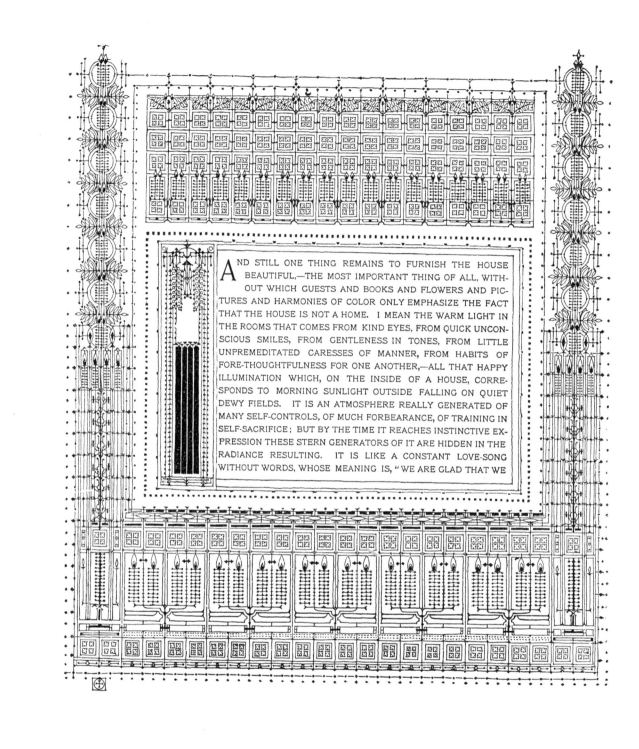

A ND STILL ONE THING REMAINS TO FURNISH THE HOUSE BEAUTIFUL,—THE MOST IMPORTANT THING OF ALL, WITHOUT WHICH GUESTS AND BOOKS AND FLOWERS AND PICTURES AND HARMONIES OF COLOR ONLY EMPHASIZE THE FACT THAT THE HOUSE IS NOT A HOME. I MEAN THE WARM LIGHT IN THE ROOMS THAT COMES FROM KIND EYES, FROM QUICK UNCONSCIOUS SMILES, FROM GENTLENESS IN TONES, FROM LITTLE UNPREMEDITATED CARESSES OF MANNER, FROM HABITS OF FORE-THOUGHTFULNESS FOR ONE ANOTHER,—ALL THAT HAPPY ILLUMINATION WHICH, ON THE INSIDE OF A HOUSE, CORRESPONDS TO MORNING SUNLIGHT OUTSIDE FALLING ON QUIET DEWY FIELDS. IT IS AN ATMOSPHERE REALLY GENERATED OF MANY SELF-CONTROLS, OF MUCH FORBEARANCE, OF TRAINING IN SELF-SACRIFICE; BUT BY THE TIME IT REACHES INSTINCTIVE EXPRESSION THESE STERN GENERATORS OF IT ARE HIDDEN IN THE RADIANCE RESULTING. IT IS LIKE A CONSTANT LOVE-SONG WITHOUT WORDS, WHOSE MEANING IS, "WE ARE GLAD THAT WE

THE HOUSE BEAUTIFUL
CHAPTER SIX
THE DEAR TOGETHERNESS."

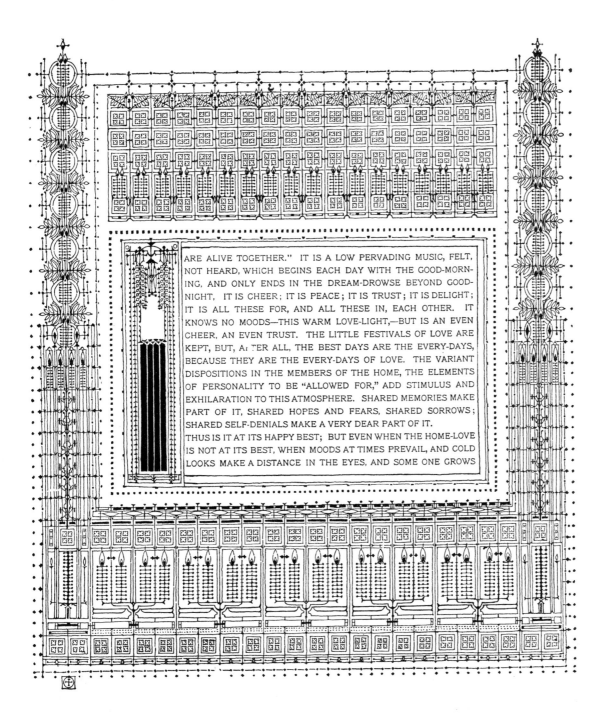

ARE ALIVE TOGETHER." IT IS A LOW PERVADING MUSIC, FELT, NOT HEARD, WHICH BEGINS EACH DAY WITH THE GOOD-MORN-ING, AND ONLY ENDS IN THE DREAM-DROWSE BEYOND GOOD-NIGHT. IT IS CHEER; IT IS PEACE; IT IS TRUST; IT IS DELIGHT; IT IS ALL THESE FOR, AND ALL THESE IN, EACH OTHER. IT KNOWS NO MOODS—THIS WARM LOVE-LIGHT,—BUT IS AN EVEN CHEER, AN EVEN TRUST. THE LITTLE FESTIVALS OF LOVE ARE KEPT, BUT, AFTER ALL, THE BEST DAYS ARE THE EVERY-DAYS, BECAUSE THEY ARE THE EVERY-DAYS OF LOVE. THE VARIANT DISPOSITIONS IN THE MEMBERS OF THE HOME, THE ELEMENTS OF PERSONALITY TO BE "ALLOWED FOR," ADD STIMULUS AND EXHILARATION TO THIS ATMOSPHERE. SHARED MEMORIES MAKE PART OF IT, SHARED HOPES AND FEARS, SHARED SORROWS; SHARED SELF-DENIALS MAKE A VERY DEAR PART OF IT.

THUS IS IT AT ITS HAPPY BEST; BUT EVEN WHEN THE HOME-LOVE IS NOT AT ITS BEST, WHEN MOODS AT TIMES PREVAIL, AND COLD LOOKS MAKE A DISTANCE IN THE EYES, AND SOME ONE GROWS

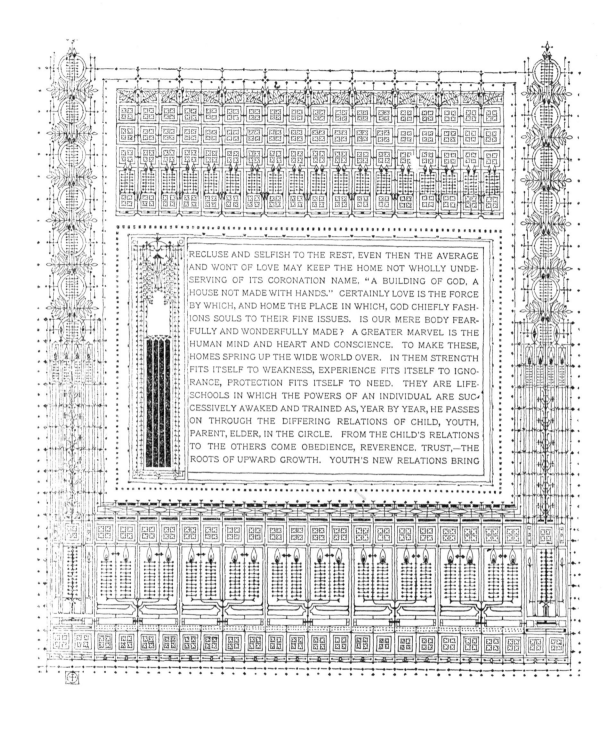

RECLUSE AND SELFISH TO THE REST, EVEN THEN THE AVERAGE
AND WONT OF LOVE MAY KEEP THE HOME NOT WHOLLY UNDE-
SERVING OF ITS CORONATION NAME. "A BUILDING OF GOD, A
HOUSE NOT MADE WITH HANDS." CERTAINLY LOVE IS THE FORCE
BY WHICH, AND HOME THE PLACE IN WHICH, GOD CHIEFLY FASH-
IONS SOULS TO THEIR FINE ISSUES. IS OUR MERE BODY FEAR-
FULLY AND WONDERFULLY MADE? A GREATER MARVEL IS THE
HUMAN MIND AND HEART AND CONSCIENCE. TO MAKE THESE,
HOMES SPRING UP THE WIDE WORLD OVER. IN THEM STRENGTH
FITS ITSELF TO WEAKNESS, EXPERIENCE FITS ITSELF TO IGNO-
RANCE, PROTECTION FITS ITSELF TO NEED. THEY ARE LIFE-
SCHOOLS IN WHICH THE POWERS OF AN INDIVIDUAL ARE SUC-
CESSIVELY AWAKED AND TRAINED AS, YEAR BY YEAR, HE PASSES
ON THROUGH THE DIFFERING RELATIONS OF CHILD, YOUTH,
PARENT, ELDER, IN THE CIRCLE. FROM THE CHILD'S RELATIONS
TO THE OTHERS COME OBEDIENCE, REVERENCE, TRUST,—THE
ROOTS OF UPWARD GROWTH. YOUTH'S NEW RELATIONS BRING

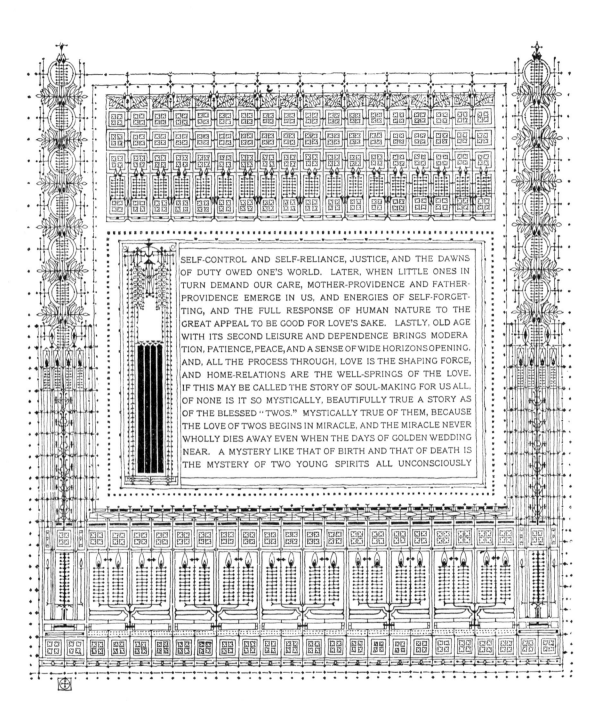

SELF-CONTROL AND SELF-RELIANCE, JUSTICE, AND THE DAWNS OF DUTY OWED ONE'S WORLD. LATER, WHEN LITTLE ONES IN TURN DEMAND OUR CARE, MOTHER-PROVIDENCE AND FATHER-PROVIDENCE EMERGE IN US, AND ENERGIES OF SELF-FORGETTING, AND THE FULL RESPONSE OF HUMAN NATURE TO THE GREAT APPEAL TO BE GOOD FOR LOVE'S SAKE. LASTLY, OLD AGE WITH ITS SECOND LEISURE AND DEPENDENCE BRINGS MODERATION, PATIENCE, PEACE, AND A SENSE OF WIDE HORIZONS OPENING. AND, ALL THE PROCESS THROUGH, LOVE IS THE SHAPING FORCE, AND HOME-RELATIONS ARE THE WELL-SPRINGS OF THE LOVE. IF THIS MAY BE CALLED THE STORY OF SOUL-MAKING FOR US ALL, OF NONE IS IT SO MYSTICALLY, BEAUTIFULLY TRUE A STORY AS OF THE BLESSED "TWOS." MYSTICALLY TRUE OF THEM, BECAUSE THE LOVE OF TWOS BEGINS IN MIRACLE, AND THE MIRACLE NEVER WHOLLY DIES AWAY EVEN WHEN THE DAYS OF GOLDEN WEDDING NEAR. A MYSTERY LIKE THAT OF BIRTH AND THAT OF DEATH IS THE MYSTERY OF TWO YOUNG SPIRITS ALL UNCONSCIOUSLY

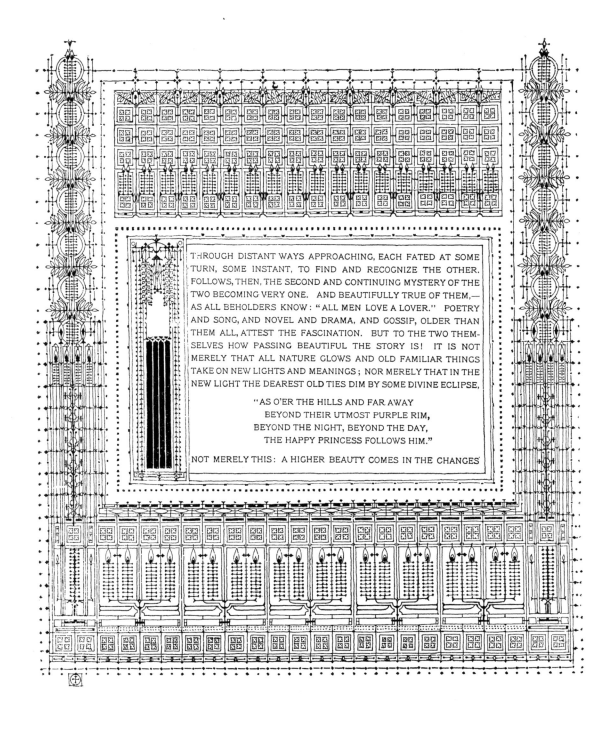

THROUGH DISTANT WAYS APPROACHING, EACH FATED AT SOME
TURN, SOME INSTANT, TO FIND AND RECOGNIZE THE OTHER.
FOLLOWS, THEN, THE SECOND AND CONTINUING MYSTERY OF THE
TWO BECOMING VERY ONE. AND BEAUTIFULLY TRUE OF THEM,—
AS ALL BEHOLDERS KNOW: "ALL MEN LOVE A LOVER." POETRY
AND SONG, AND NOVEL AND DRAMA, AND GOSSIP, OLDER THAN
THEM ALL, ATTEST THE FASCINATION. BUT TO THE TWO THEM-
SELVES HOW PASSING BEAUTIFUL THE STORY IS! IT IS NOT
MERELY THAT ALL NATURE GLOWS AND OLD FAMILIAR THINGS
TAKE ON NEW LIGHTS AND MEANINGS ; NOR MERELY THAT IN THE
NEW LIGHT THE DEAREST OLD TIES DIM BY SOME DIVINE ECLIPSE,

"AS O'ER THE HILLS AND FAR AWAY
BEYOND THEIR UTMOST PURPLE RIM,
BEYOND THE NIGHT, BEYOND THE DAY,
THE HAPPY PRINCESS FOLLOWS HIM."

NOT MERELY THIS: A HIGHER BEAUTY COMES IN THE CHANGES

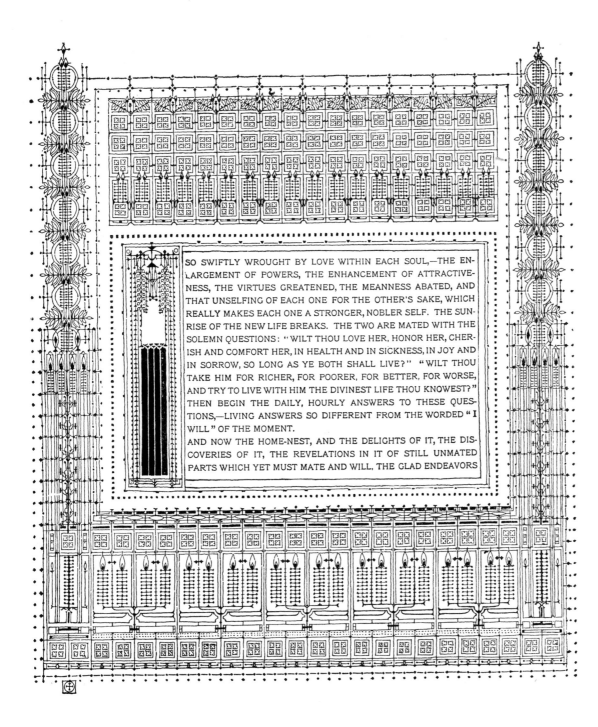

SO SWIFTLY WROUGHT BY LOVE WITHIN EACH SOUL,—THE EN-
LARGEMENT OF POWERS, THE ENHANCEMENT OF ATTRACTIVE-
NESS, THE VIRTUES GREATENED, THE MEANNESS ABATED, AND
THAT UNSELFING OF EACH ONE FOR THE OTHER'S SAKE, WHICH
REALLY MAKES EACH ONE A STRONGER, NOBLER SELF. THE SUN-
RISE OF THE NEW LIFE BREAKS. THE TWO ARE MATED WITH THE
SOLEMN QUESTIONS: "WILT THOU LOVE HER, HONOR HER, CHER-
ISH AND COMFORT HER, IN HEALTH AND IN SICKNESS, IN JOY AND
IN SORROW, SO LONG AS YE BOTH SHALL LIVE?" "WILT THOU
TAKE HIM FOR RICHER, FOR POORER, FOR BETTER, FOR WORSE,
AND TRY TO LIVE WITH HIM THE DIVINEST LIFE THOU KNOWEST?"
THEN BEGIN THE DAILY, HOURLY ANSWERS TO THESE QUES-
TIONS,—LIVING ANSWERS SO DIFFERENT FROM THE WORDED "I
WILL" OF THE MOMENT.
AND NOW THE HOME-NEST, AND THE DELIGHTS OF IT, THE DIS-
COVERIES OF IT, THE REVELATIONS IN IT OF STILL UNMATED
PARTS WHICH YET MUST MATE AND WILL, THE GLAD ENDEAVORS

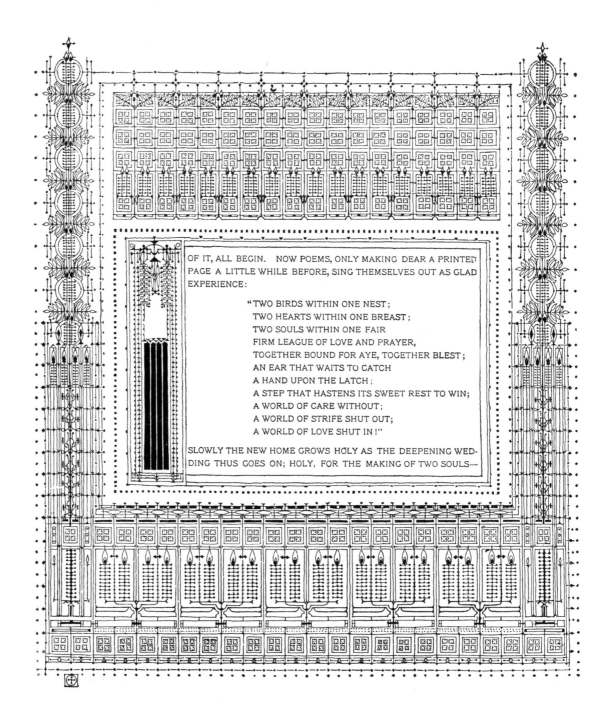

OF IT, ALL BEGIN. NOW POEMS, ONLY MAKING DEAR A PRINTED PAGE A LITTLE WHILE BEFORE, SING THEMSELVES OUT AS GLAD EXPERIENCE:

"TWO BIRDS WITHIN ONE NEST;
TWO HEARTS WITHIN ONE BREAST;
TWO SOULS WITHIN ONE FAIR
FIRM LEAGUE OF LOVE AND PRAYER,
TOGETHER BOUND FOR AYE, TOGETHER BLEST;
AN EAR THAT WAITS TO CATCH
A HAND UPON THE LATCH;
A STEP THAT HASTENS ITS SWEET REST TO WIN;
A WORLD OF CARE WITHOUT;
A WORLD OF STRIFE SHUT OUT;
A WORLD OF LOVE SHUT IN!"

SLOWLY THE NEW HOME GROWS HOLY AS THE DEEPENING WEDDING THUS GOES ON; HOLY, FOR THE MAKING OF TWO SOULS—

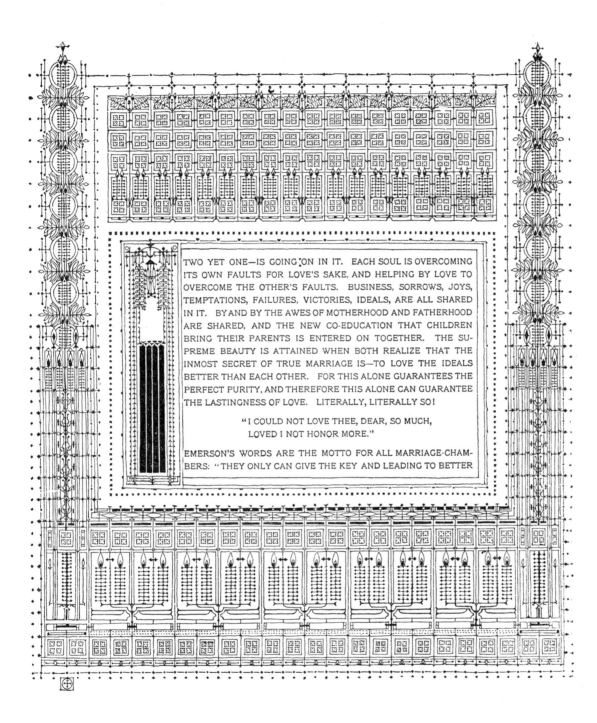

TWO YET ONE—IS GOING ON IN IT. EACH SOUL IS OVERCOMING ITS OWN FAULTS FOR LOVE'S SAKE, AND HELPING BY LOVE TO OVERCOME THE OTHER'S FAULTS. BUSINESS, SORROWS, JOYS, TEMPTATIONS, FAILURES, VICTORIES, IDEALS, ARE ALL SHARED IN IT. BY AND BY THE AWES OF MOTHERHOOD AND FATHERHOOD ARE SHARED, AND THE NEW CO-EDUCATION THAT CHILDREN BRING THEIR PARENTS IS ENTERED ON TOGETHER. THE SUPREME BEAUTY IS ATTAINED WHEN BOTH REALIZE THAT THE INMOST SECRET OF TRUE MARRIAGE IS—TO LOVE THE IDEALS BETTER THAN EACH OTHER. FOR THIS ALONE GUARANTEES THE PERFECT PURITY, AND THEREFORE THIS ALONE CAN GUARANTEE THE LASTINGNESS OF LOVE. LITERALLY, LITERALLY SO!

"I COULD NOT LOVE THEE, DEAR, SO MUCH,
LOVED I NOT HONOR MORE."

EMERSON'S WORDS ARE THE MOTTO FOR ALL MARRIAGE-CHAMBERS: "THEY ONLY CAN GIVE THE KEY AND LEADING TO BETTER

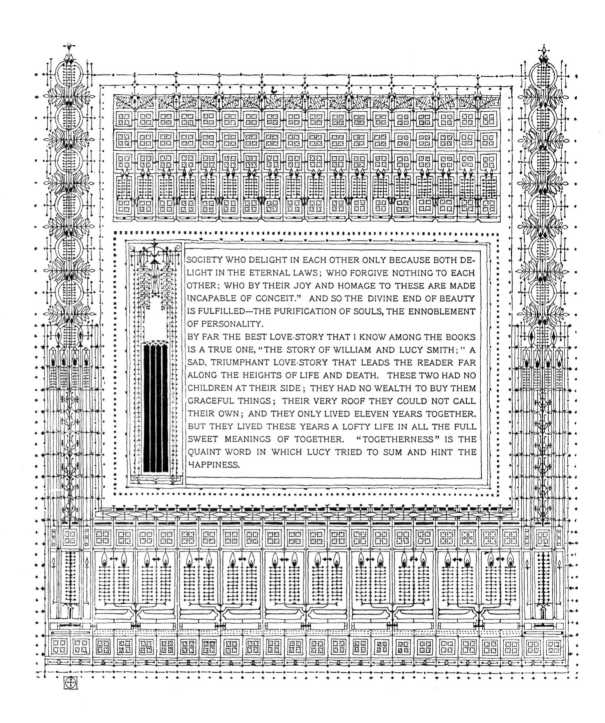

SOCIETY WHO DELIGHT IN EACH OTHER ONLY BECAUSE BOTH DE-
LIGHT IN THE ETERNAL LAWS; WHO FORGIVE NOTHING TO EACH
OTHER; WHO BY THEIR JOY AND HOMAGE TO THESE ARE MADE
INCAPABLE OF CONCEIT." AND SO THE DIVINE END OF BEAUTY
IS FULFILLED—THE PURIFICATION OF SOULS, THE ENNOBLEMENT
OF PERSONALITY.

BY FAR THE BEST LOVE-STORY THAT I KNOW AMONG THE BOOKS
IS A TRUE ONE, "THE STORY OF WILLIAM AND LUCY SMITH;" A
SAD, TRIUMPHANT LOVE-STORY THAT LEADS THE READER FAR
ALONG THE HEIGHTS OF LIFE AND DEATH. THESE TWO HAD NO
CHILDREN AT THEIR SIDE; THEY HAD NO WEALTH TO BUY THEM
GRACEFUL THINGS; THEIR VERY ROOF THEY COULD NOT CALL
THEIR OWN; AND THEY ONLY LIVED ELEVEN YEARS TOGETHER.
BUT THEY LIVED THESE YEARS A LOFTY LIFE IN ALL THE FULL
SWEET MEANINGS OF TOGETHER. "TOGETHERNESS" IS THE
QUAINT WORD IN WHICH LUCY TRIED TO SUM AND HINT THE
HAPPINESS.

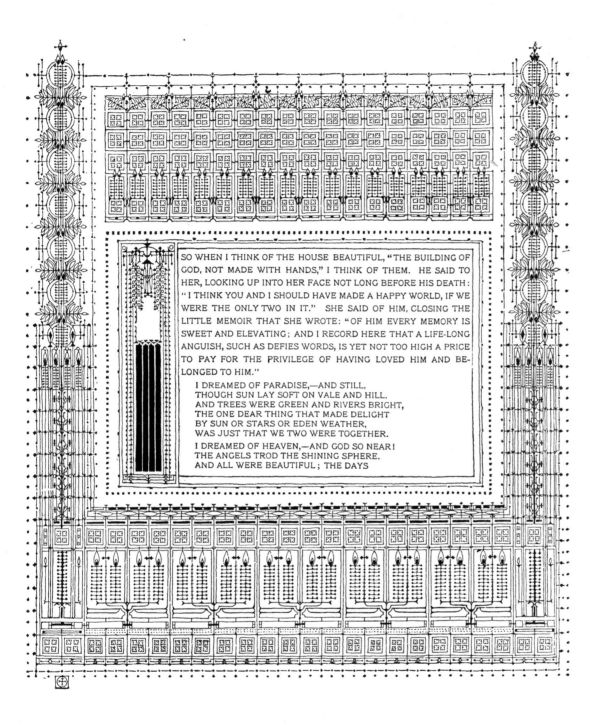

SO WHEN I THINK OF THE HOUSE BEAUTIFUL, "THE BUILDING OF GOD, NOT MADE WITH HANDS," I THINK OF THEM. HE SAID TO HER, LOOKING UP INTO HER FACE NOT LONG BEFORE HIS DEATH: "I THINK YOU AND I SHOULD HAVE MADE A HAPPY WORLD, IF WE WERE THE ONLY TWO IN IT." SHE SAID OF HIM, CLOSING THE LITTLE MEMOIR THAT SHE WROTE: "OF HIM EVERY MEMORY IS SWEET AND ELEVATING; AND I RECORD HERE THAT A LIFE-LONG ANGUISH, SUCH AS DEFIES WORDS, IS YET NOT TOO HIGH A PRICE TO PAY FOR THE PRIVILEGE OF HAVING LOVED HIM AND BE-LONGED TO HIM."

I DREAMED OF PARADISE,—AND STILL,
THOUGH SUN LAY SOFT ON VALE AND HILL,
AND TREES WERE GREEN AND RIVERS BRIGHT,
THE ONE DEAR THING THAT MADE DELIGHT
BY SUN OR STARS OR EDEN WEATHER,
WAS JUST THAT WE TWO WERE TOGETHER.

I DREAMED OF HEAVEN,—AND GOD SO NEAR!
THE ANGELS TROD THE SHINING SPHERE.
AND ALL WERE BEAUTIFUL; THE DAYS

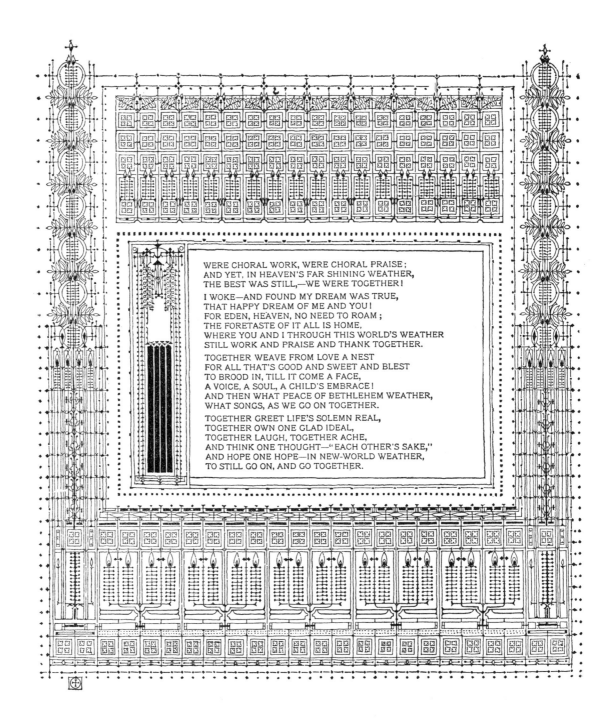

WERE CHORAL WORK, WERE CHORAL PRAISE;
AND YET, IN HEAVEN'S FAR SHINING WEATHER,
THE BEST WAS STILL,—WE WERE TOGETHER!

I WOKE—AND FOUND MY DREAM WAS TRUE,
THAT HAPPY DREAM OF ME AND YOU!
FOR EDEN, HEAVEN, NO NEED TO ROAM;
THE FORETASTE OF IT ALL IS HOME,
WHERE YOU AND I THROUGH THIS WORLD'S WEATHER
STILL WORK AND PRAISE AND THANK TOGETHER.

TOGETHER WEAVE FROM LOVE A NEST
FOR ALL THAT'S GOOD AND SWEET AND BLEST
TO BROOD IN, TILL IT COME A FACE,
A VOICE, A SOUL, A CHILD'S EMBRACE!
AND THEN WHAT PEACE OF BETHLEHEM WEATHER,
WHAT SONGS, AS WE GO ON TOGETHER.

TOGETHER GREET LIFE'S SOLEMN REAL,
TOGETHER OWN ONE GLAD IDEAL,
TOGETHER LAUGH, TOGETHER ACHE,
AND THINK ONE THOUGHT—"EACH OTHER'S SAKE,"
AND HOPE ONE HOPE—IN NEW-WORLD WEATHER,
TO STILL GO ON, AND GO TOGETHER.

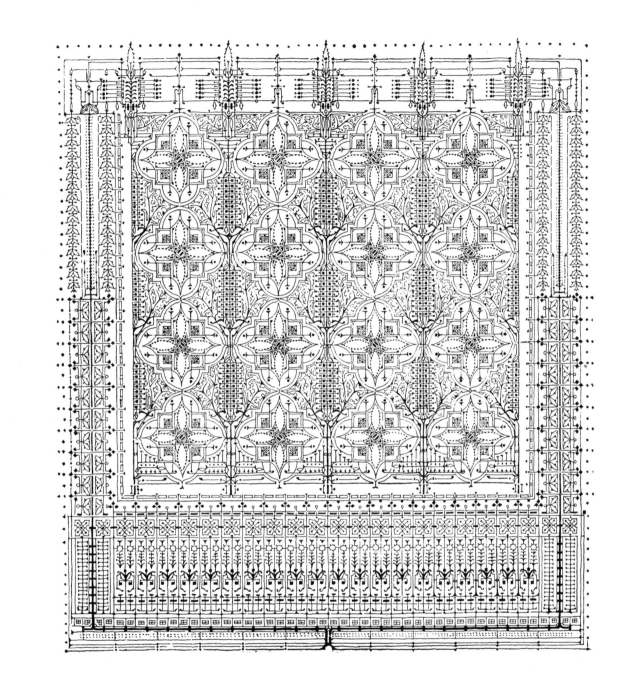

AUVERGNE PRESS

WE HAVE PRINTED NINETY COPIES OF
THIS BOOK.   THIS IS COPY NO. *Eighteen*

W. H. Winslow.

Frank L. Wright.